THE REVISED VERSION

EDITED FOR THE USE OF SCHOOLS

JOEL, OBADIAH,
JONAH AND MALACHI

JOEL, OBADIAH, JONAH AND MALACHI

BY

T. H. HENNESSY, M.A.

RECTOR OF FULBOURN, CAMBRIDGE
FORMERLY DEAN AND LECTURER OF SELWYN COLLEGE,
CAMBRIDGE

CAMBRIDGE

AT THE UNIVERSITY PRESS

1919

CAMBRIDGE
UNIVERSITY PRESS

University Printing House, Cambridge CB2 8BS, United Kingdom

Published in the United States of America by Cambridge University Press, New York

Cambridge University Press is part of the University of Cambridge.

It furthers the University's mission by disseminating knowledge in the pursuit of education, learning and research at the highest international levels of excellence.

www.cambridge.org
Information on this title: www.cambridge.org/9781107642034

© Cambridge University Press 1919

First published 1919
First paperback edition 2014

A catalogue record for this publication is available from the British Library

ISBN 978-1-107-64203-4 Paperback

PREFACE BY THE GENERAL EDITOR
FOR THE OLD TESTAMENT

THE aim of this series of commentaries is to explain the Revised Version for young students, and at the same time to present, in a simple form, the main results of the best scholarship of the day.

The general editor has confined himself to supervision and suggestion. The writer is, in each case, responsible for the opinions expressed and for the treatment of particular passages.

A. H. M^CNEILE.

March, 1919.

CONTENTS

ABBREVIATIONS, ETC.

A.V. The Authorised Version of the English Bible set forth 1611.

b The second part of a verse.

cf. compare.

chap. chapter.

Diod. Diodorus Siculus, the historian (1st century B.C.).

f. following verse.

ff. following verses.

Hebrew original or Mass. Text. The Hebrew text of the O.T. as handed down by the Massoretes (6th to 10th centuries A.D.).

i.e. that is to say.

in loco comment on the same passage.

Jos. *Ant. The Antiquities of the Jews,* by Josephus.

LXX The translation of the Old Testament into Greek, commonly called the Septuagint. LXX A = Codex Alexandrinus. LXX B = Codex Vaticanus.

marg. margin.

MS Manuscript.

N.T. The New Testament Scriptures.

O.T. The Old Testament Scriptures.

p. page.

pp. pages.

Peshitta The translation of the Scriptures into Syriac.

R.V. The Revised Version of the English Bible.

sc. To be understood, *or* meaning.

Targums The paraphrases in Aramaic of parts of the Old Testament.

vv. verses.

viz. namely.

Vulgate or Vulg. The translation of the Scriptures into Latin.

THE

BOOK OF JOEL

INTRODUCTION

§ 1. THE PROPHET JOEL.

The name Joel has been thought to be the name of a god which is apparently found on Phoenician inscriptions. Others consider it to mean 'the strong-willed' or 'the refuge.' The usual and the most probable interpretation is ' Jehovah is God ' which is the expression of a fundamental article of the O.T. Prophets' creed, and is also the meaning of the name Elijah. The name occurs very frequently in the Old Testament Scriptures. It was borne by thirteen, if not fourteen, persons, of whom the best known, apart from the prophet, was Joel, the elder son of Samuel (1 Sam. viii. 2).

We know nothing about Joel except what may be gathered from his prophecy. He was the son of Pethuel (or Bethuel, according to the LXX and other versions). The latter name was that of Nahor's son the nephew of Abraham and father of Laban and Rebekah (Gen. xxii. 22). Nothing else is known of Pethuel.

As Joel's interest centres in Jerusalem and Judah and he displays familiarity with the Temple and the service of the priests, it is a fair inference that he was a native of Judah. When he uses the name Israel (ii. 27, iii. 2, 16), apparently it is in the wider sense and includes the whole of God's chosen people. With the possible exception of iii. 2 he does not use it in the narrower sense of the Northern Kingdom alone. It has been thought that, like Jeremiah and Ezekiel, he was himself a priest; but in the absence of an express statement, this must remain doubtful.

§ 2. THE OCCASION AND CONTENTS OF THE PROPHECY.

The occasion of the prophecy was apparently a visitation of locusts of unusual severity. It lasted for more than a year (see ii. 25), and was accompanied by an unparalleled drought which reduced the land to desolation. Man and beast are in despair. There is no food, no water to drink; and the enforced cessation of the daily offerings in the Temple seems to suggest the thought that communion between Jehovah and His people has been—at least temporarily—interrupted.

The prophecy consists of two parts:—i. 1—ii. 17 and ii. 18—end.

i. 1—ii. 17 are the words of the prophet. They embrace two discourses. The first discourse in chap. i. gives a vivid description of the locust plague and the drought. In the second discourse (c. ii. 1— 17) there is an equally graphic description of the onset of the locusts, and the prophet adds an earnest appeal to the people to turn to Jehovah with sincere repentance (vv. 12—14), and concludes with a call to a public service of supplication. A solemn litany of intercession is put forth which shall be offered in the Temple court.

The second part of the book (ii. 18—end) contains Jehovah's answer to His people's prayer. Apparently the call to repentance has been obeyed, and the people's supplication has been accepted. The answer of Jehovah falls into three parts. In vv. 18—27 the removal of the plagues, abundance of rain and increased fertility of the soil are promised. This is followed in *vv*. 28—32 by a promise of the realization of Moses' wish (see Num. xi. 29), the outpouring of Jehovah's spirit upon all flesh, so that the great and terrible day of Jehovah, when it comes, will be a day of judgement upon Israel's foes and a day of deliverance for those who 'shall call on the name of Jehovah.' The third part of Jehovah's answer is chapter iii. The nations are summoned to the valley of Jehoshaphat to be judged. The issue will be that Jehovah will be a 'refuge unto His people and a stronghold to the children of Israel.' He will dwell in Zion His holy mountain in the midst of His pardoned and sanctified people.

The following analysis may be of use:

I.	c. i.—ii. 17.	Two prophetic discourses.
	(i) i. 1—20.	The locust plague and drought.
	(ii) ii. 1—17.	The onset of the locusts (*vv*. 1—11); a call to repentance (*vv*. 12—17).
II.	c. ii. 18—end.	Jehovah's answer.
	(i) ii. 18—27.	Promise of material blessings.
	(ii) ii. 28—32.	Promise of spiritual blessings before the Day of Jehovah.
	(iii) iii. 1—15.	Judgement of the nations.
	(iv) iii. 16—end.	Purified Jerusalem rejoicing in the Presence of Jehovah.

§ 3. The Character of the Prophecy.

The pre-exilic prophets of the O.T. dealt with the circumstances of their own day.   Their object was to trace the dealings of Jehovah with His people in what was happening at the time.   Sometimes they offer words of faith and hope, especially when a hostile power is threatening Israel.   At other times words of rebuke are necessary, chiefly in days of prosperity when the moral ideal is lowered and the old temptations to idolatry are no longer resisted.

As a consequence it is easy from the writings of such prophets as Hosea, Isaiah, and Jeremiah to deduce what were the social, moral, and religious conditions in which they lived.   And there is no doubt that the conditions set forth in these prophecies are to be understood as *literal* and *historical*.

In later days, however, another method of presenting religious teaching gradually came into vogue. The Babylonian exile brought with it a new outlook for Israel's religious teachers. The lessons of the past and present gave place to thoughts about the future. In the course of time a consciousness grew up that some great catastrophic judgement was impending which would usher in a New Age not only for Israel but for all the world. The thought, at least in some respects, was no new one. It had been present, though but dimly and in a subordinate degree, in the minds of the pre-exilic prophets (see Amos v. 18; Is. ii. 11—17, xiii. 6, 9; Zeph. i. 14, ii. 2). Israel's contact with the Graeco-Roman world in the 2nd century B.C. extended the mental vision of its thinkers and, as has been well said, ' from Maccabaean days the Jews "learned to think imperially." ' The Book of Daniel is a product of this century, and it is only the first of a series of similar books which saw the light during the course of the second and subsequent century before Christ. The writers of these Apocalyptic books (as they are called) regarded the world as a whole. The great world-powers were now seen to have each its appointed part in the evolution of the Kingdom of God, of which (as has been said) the advent would be preceded by a universal catastrophic upheaval embracing all mankind and even the whole of nature.

The book of Joel has a close resemblance to the imagery of this apocalyptic literature. The question therefore immediately arises, Is the Book of Joel an *apocalypse*? All that will be attempted here in reference to this question, which is still undetermined, is to set out what has been urged on both sides. In favour of the apocalyptic nature of Joel's prophecy it has been urged that (1) the locusts are not *actual* locusts. They are strange supernatural creatures; and the description of them is not to be understood literally any more than the singular description of locusts in Rev. ix., an acknowledged apocalyptic writing. (2) The army of c. ii. cannot be a description of creatures of flesh and blood. They are a mysterious host of unearthly warriors. (3) The expression 'the Day of Jehovah' is a well-known expression in apocalyptic literature. (4) The term 'Northerner' in ii. 20 is a technical expression used in Israel from the days of Jeremiah to express the instruments of Jehovah's wrath in the day of His Judgement. It was practically equivalent to Doom.

On the other hand the following considerations have been urged. (1) There is no hint that Joel is addressing any one except his immediate contemporaries. (2) In i. 16 he places himself amongst his hearers as experiencing their sufferings and privations. (3) The locust army of c. ii. is to be identified with the locusts of c. i. which are undoubtedly *actual* locusts. The setting of c. ii. is sufficiently accounted for by the awfulness of the actual plague, the terribleness of the evil of which the plague is a foreshadowing, to say nothing of the allowance for poetic hyperbole or idealism. (4) ii. 21—25 can hardly be understood otherwise than literally. (5) Also it is difficult, if not impossible, to explain the call to repentance (ii. 12—17) in any other than a literal and historical sense. The same remark also applies to ii. 18, 19. (6) Joel's figures are too vivid and too actual to be merely predictive, mystical, or apocalyptic.

Another mode of interpretation is the *allegorical*, which commended itself to many of the early Christian Fathers. According to this interpretation an actual human army is described under the figure of locusts and these locusts are to be identified with the nations mentioned in c. iii. It is not clear on this interpretation, if, in the prophet's time, the invasion and subsequent devastation are already past occurrences, or if they are still what the future has in store for Israel. Both ideas have found advocates. Those who accept the allegorical interpretation urge the following considerations:—(1) the description of the locusts in cc. i. and ii. much exceeds the bounds of possible reality; (2) mere locusts could not possibly produce the effects mentioned in i. 9, ii. 25; (3) such expressions as 'nation' (i. 6), 'the nations should rule over them' (ii. 17), 'he hath done great things' (ii. 20) clearly cannot be applied to irrational locusts. They are applicable only to human beings. (4) Invading armies are usually represented as attacking from the North (see ii. 20, cf. Is. x. 28, xiv. 31; Jer. i. 13 ff.) whereas locust-swarms never invade Palestine from that quarter. (5) The four kinds of locusts (i. 4, ii. 25) symbolize four successive invasions, or four empires to which Israel was subject (cf. Dan. ii. and vii.). (6) ii. 20 cannot refer to locusts. It is an emblem of the fate of a human invader.

To these arguments the following answers have been made. (1) The prophecy of Joel is not bare prose; it is poetry. Consequently hyperbole is to be expected and due allowance must accordingly be made. This is a sufficient explanation for the language used in i. 2, i. 6, i. 19, ii. 1—11, ii. 20. With regard to ii. 17 the translation given in the R.V. margin is, to say the least, equally admissible. (2) It must be borne in mind that the devastation which locust-swarms have been known to work far exceed what might be expected. (3) The locusts of c. i. are not identified with the Day of Jehovah. They are but a symbol of its approach. (4) The essential characteristic of an allegory is that the thing signifying and the thing signified interpenetrate and blend together so closely that the qualities and properties of the first are *attributed* to the last. In ii. 1—11 this is not the case. The locusts are *compared* with a body of warriors (see ii. 4, 5, 7). (5) It is surely too strong an assertion to say that locusts *never* enter Palestine from the north.

There remains the *literal* interpretation of the prophecy. The chief points, which satisfy those who adopt it, are: (1) A visitation of locusts accompanied by a drought called forth the prophecy. To Joel these suggested the great and terrible day of Jehovah, which is described with prophetic idealism. Israel, now that it has sincerely repented, will be justified in that day and its enemies destroyed. (2) The description of the visitation answers to that of a plague of actual locusts and not to that of a human invasion. For there is no reference to any slaying or looting or other horrors inseparable from warfare.

These, then, are the three different interpretations which have hitherto been offered. It has lately been suggested that the original prophecy of Joel had reference to an actual locust-plague and that it has been re-edited once if not twice by those imbued with apocalyptic ideas and so the whole character of the original prophecy has been altered so as to become something in the nature of an apocalypse.

§ 4. THE DATE OF JOEL.

When did Joel write his prophecy? The answers which have been given to this question generally assign one of two periods to its composition, either (a) the reign of Jehoash, king of Judah B.C. 837—801, or (b) a period after the exile. The last years of Josiah B.C. 640—608 have also been suggested, chiefly on the grounds, (i) that the drought of Joel i. 17—20 is to be identified with that referred to in Jer. xiv. 2—6; (ii) that the expression 'the northerner' in Joel ii. 20 points to this date (see Jer. i. 14, iv. 6, vi. 1, x. 22); and (iii) that certain phrases in Joel ii. 12, 13 imply a period of apostasy. These arguments, however, have not carried conviction to the minds of many critics.

No external evidence is available. Consequently a judgement can be formed only on internal evidence, i.e. what may be deduced from the contents of the prophecy itself.

Those who favour the earlier period do so on the following grounds:

(1) iii. 19 is regarded as an allusion to the invasion of Shishak king of Egypt in the reign of Rehoboam (1 K. xiv. 25, 26), and to the revolt of Edom from

under the hand of Judah in the days of Jehoram
(2 K. viii. 20—22).

(2) The allusions to plundering by Tyre, Zidon and
the Philistines in iii. 4—6 are held to be the plunder
recorded in 2 Chron. xxi. 16, 17, xxii. 1. Further Amos
(i. 6, 9) says that Gaza and Tyre traded in Jewish slaves.

(3) Jehoash of Judah was only seven years old at
his accession (2 K. xi. 21), and the control of affairs was
mainly in the hands of the priest Jehoiada (2 K. xi. 4 ff.).
This accounts for the absence of the mention of a king
and the prominent position of elders and priests in the
prophecy of Joel (Joel i. 9, 13, 14, ii. 16, 17).

(4) The prophet's representations are vague,
especially that of the Day of Jehovah. His horror,
also, of the interruption of the daily offering is remarkable. These indicate the simplicity of the earlier
stages of Israel's religion.

(5) The fierce feeling displayed in the prophecy
towards other nations (iii. 1 ff.) is of a piece with the
temper of the times of the Judges and of David.

(6) No one but a member of a purely agricultural
community, such as Israel was before the 8th century
B.C., would be so absorbed in the ravages of locusts.

(7) The prophet's unwillingness to name the
Assyrians, who are symbolized by the locusts, is
shared by the 8th century prophet Amos. The
absence, therefore, of the mention of the Assyrians
by name is not an insuperable difficulty.

(8) The absence of all mention of the Law.

(9) The valley of Jehoshaphat (iii. 2, 12) is a
reference to the victory of the king of that name in
the valley of Beracah (2 Chron. xx.).

(10) Joel stands second between Hosea and Amos
in the Hebrew Canon of the so-called 'Minor' Prophets
amongst the pre-exilic prophets.

On the other hand the main arguments in support of a post-exilic date for the prophecy are the following:

(1)   Whatever the exact translation is, the phrase 'bring again the captivity' in iii. 1 means elsewhere nothing short of restoration from great national disaster, especially from the exile. At any rate iii. 2 can refer only to the Babylonian exile.

(2)   The religious and spiritual circumstances which are portrayed in the prophecy are those of post-exilic times. The nation is united religiously. The prophet betrays no such fear of the abuse of fasting and ceremonial practices as the pre-exilic prophets felt.

(3)   There is no allusion to idolatry, social disorders, maladministration of justice, oppression of the poor, which are so persistent features in the pre-exilic prophecies.

(4)   The absence of allusion to a king, and the prominence given to the priests and Temple services would at least equally—if not better—suit post-exilic days. Further iii. 4—6, the last part of iii. 17, and iii. 19 seem to point to a time after the exile. Edom exhibited particularly violent hostility at the destruction of Jerusalem (cf. Ps. cxxxvii. 7).

(5)   The limitation of the promises to Judah (see iii. 1, 18—20).

(6)   The language, style, and ideas of the prophecy, e.g. the outpouring of the spirit, Jehovah's pleading with the nations, a stream issuing from the Temple, have closer affinities with later than with earlier prophecies.

(7)   The mention of traffic with the Grecians in iii. 6. It is unlikely that Tyre had enslaved *Judæans* before the exile.

(8)   The reference to angels, if that is the meaning of 'mighty ones' in iii. 11, is conclusive of a late date.

(9) In ii. 16 the term 'the people' is apparently
coextensive with the term 'the congregation.'

The picture of the community addressed in the
prophecy has led some scholars to place Joel about
400 B.C. It is an agricultural community who exist
for the worship of Jehovah. They gather themselves
together to Zion to implore Jehovah's pity. The
future to which they are instructed to look forward is
not that of a great world-empire. It is that of a fuller
and unrestricted spiritual outpouring. Jerusalem, as a
witness of the refreshing and sustaining Presence of
God in Israel, will not again be desecrated by the feet
of foreigners. The fertility of the land will be a constant
reminder of Jehovah's care of His people as in the past
so throughout the future ages. This picture is regarded
as bearing a close resemblance to that of the Jewish community as depicted in the books of Ezra and Nehemiah
and the prophecies of Haggai and Zechariah i.—viii.
Whilst there can be little doubt that Joel is post-exilic, it
is impossible to say definitely to what period it refers.

§ 5. THE TEACHING OF JOEL.

The religious teaching in the prophecy of Joel finds
expression chiefly in connexion with the following
prominent ideas :

(1) *The day of Jehovah*. The conception is a
frequent one in the prophetical writings of the O.T.
(see note on i. 15). The prophet, as he contemplates
the devastation caused by locust-plagues or the
desolation and misery brought about by the tyranny
of brute force, sees with clear spiritual insight that
in and through such disasters the Unseen Presence
of God may be more fully realized. In the one case
when the regular succession of rain and crops, prayers
and sacrifices ceases, those whose minds have become
dulled by the very regularity may haply be driven to

see that the Invisible Cause of their life and sustenance is not Nature but a Loving Being who controls both the outward and inward orders. Hence the Day of Jehovah is a deliverance from the curse of a practical Atheism, which is a far greater plague than that of locusts or foreign oppression.   In every age, in every society, and in every heart there are experiences which answer to the prophet's conception of 'the day of the Lord.' And according to the response of every man's heart, whether he is aware of the meaning of his experience or not, his experience brings with it a day of decision (see Joel iii. 14).

(2) *The outpouring of the Spirit.* The manifold ideas attached to the use of the word 'spirit' in the O.T. are remarked upon in the note on ii. 28.

The prophet evidently declines to separate the thought of material blessings from that of spiritual endowment.   The one is an outward and visible sign of the other. It is also a witness that man needs and is capable of receiving God's Spirit. By the Spirit man is enabled to 'dream dreams and see visions,' that is to say, obtain a closer contact with realities and hold a more inward communion with Him who is the Truth—the Word of God.   St Peter (see Acts ii. 14 ff.) realized that the Spirit which was poured out at Pentecost was identical with the Spirit of whom Joel spoke. He knew that the Pentecostal outpouring was unique. It was also continuous. A new age-long Spiritual Dispensation was inaugurated at that time of which all previous outpourings were so many earnests or foreshadowings. Although Joel probably had no foresight of the Pentecostal outpouring, still the Spirit who spake by the prophet was aware that Joel's words were to find a unique fulfilment in the Christian Dispensation. It was therefore by no means beside the mark when St Peter found their fulfilment in the event which he witnessed on the Day of Pentecost. They are 'not a prediction of the *event* of Pentecost, but of the new order of things of which Pentecost was the first great example' (A. B. Davidson).

(3) *'The remnant'* (ii. 32). The doctrine of the Remnant is not peculiar to Joel. Its first announcement apparently was to the dejected Elijah at Horeb after the controversy on Carmel (see 1 K. xix. 18). It is found in Amos (ix. 8—10), Micah (ii. 12, iv. 7, v. 3), Zephaniah (iii. 12, 13), Jeremiah (xxiii. 3), Ezekiel (xiv. 14—20, 22), and especially in Isaiah who called his son Shear-Yashub as a witness of the truth of the doctrine (vii. 3, x. 21). The characteristic of this doctrine is that *the individual* no less than *the nation* is regarded as the subject of God's nurture and care. From a small nucleus of individuals and not from the whole nation will spring the power through which salvation will come. The idea is one which was adopted by St Peter (Acts ii. 21), St Stephen (Acts vii. 2—53), and St Paul (Rom. ix. 27). They found it true to experience.

(4) *The power of penitence.* The power of sincere and heartfelt (ii. 13) repentance is clearly taught. It appeals to God's Honour (see note on ii. 18) and to His Love, and can avail to avert further desolation and to repair the past. It also brings home to men the sense of God's abiding presence in their midst, and affords a certainty of God's incomparable nature, and confidence in His sustaining power (ii. 12—27). Outward signs of penitence are not to be abandoned; they have their place if they are tokens of inward sincerity (ii. 12, 13). Deliverance is available to anyone and everyone who puts his trust in the grace of God (ii. 32, cf. Rom. x. 13).

(5) *The dwelling of the Lord in the midst of Israel.* This important truth is mentioned three times (ii. 27,

iii. 17, 21). It is a foreshadowing of the greatest event in the world's history when 'the Word became Flesh and dwelt among us.' It is to be noticed that there is no reference to a personal Messiah throughout the prophecy. See however note on ii. 23. In the prophecy however it is connected with a narrow nationalism, which in the days of the author of Jonah began to give way to broader ideas. This nationalism served a purpose. It helped to keep alive the sense of the great and incessant conflict between good and evil. Even in the days when Israel was least conscious of its own depravity, the nations were to them the representatives of the powers of evil. Its deflection from God's standard was due rather to self-deception than to conscious wilfulness.

The prophecy has supplied imagery in which N.T. writers have clothed some of their ideas.

(*a*) 'The day of the Lord.' This prophetical idea seems to underlie the thought in 1 Cor. i. 8, v. 5; 2 Cor. i. 14; Phil. i. 6, 10, ii. 16; 1 Thess. v. 2; 2 Thess. ii. 2; 2 Pet. iii. 10, 12; Rev. xvi. 14, cf. St Luke xvii. 24. In each case it represents those manifold revelations of God to men's hearts which bring joy to the believing and dismay and terror to the godless. These manifold revelations will find their consummation in the great Final Revelation at the Last Day.

(*b*) The locusts of Rev. ix. 3 may look back to Joel i. and ii., or to Exod. x. In all three they are, or represent, a terrible scourge.

(*c*) In Rev. xiv. 15, as in Joel iii. 13, the harvest is connected with judgement; cf. also Jer. xxviii. 33, li. 33; St Matt. xiii. 39; St Mark iv. 29.

(*d*) Rev. xxii. 1 speaks of 'a river of water of life. The conception may be based on Joel iii. 18; it is found also in Zech. xiv. 8; Ezek. xlvii. 9; cf. Gen. ii. 9 ff.; Is. viii. 6; Ps. xlvi. 4; St John ix. 7.

THE

BOOK OF JOEL

THE word of the LORD that came to Joel the son 1
of Pethuel.

i. 2–4. *Unprecedented devastation by locusts.*

Hear this, ye old men, and give ear, all ye in- 2
habitants of the land. Hath this been in your days,
or in the days of your fathers? Tell ye your 3
children of it, and *let* your children *tell* their children,
and their children another generation. That which 4
the palmerworm hath left hath the locust eaten; and
that which the locust hath left hath the cankerworm eaten; and that which the cankerworm hath
left hath the caterpiller eaten.

---

1. 1. the Lord. The Hebrew word, which is here translated 'the Lord,' is the proper name by which God was
known in Israel. The pronunciation of this name is
uncertain. The nearest modern equivalent is probably
YAHWEH, see p. 36 f.

Joel. The name Joel was borne also by Samuel's first-
born son (1 Sam. viii. 2; 1 Chron. vi. 18) and many other
less conspicuous persons in the O.T. narrative.

Pethuel. The LXX seems to have read Bethuel, a name
identical with that of Abraham's nephew (Gen. xxii. 22).

2. old men. The Hebrew word is used (1) in reference
to age, and (2) technically with regard to authority, 'an
elder.' Here it is used in the former sense.

2–3. The expressions imply that the event is unparalleled and marks a turning-point in history.

4. As the Revisers point out in their margin, it is
uncertain whether different kinds of locusts are referred
to, or locusts in different stages of growth. The devastation lasted more years than one (see ii. 25).

5–13. *The severity of the devastation.*

5 Awake, ye drunkards, and weep; and howl, all ye
    drinkers of wine, because of the sweet wine; for
6 it is cut off from your mouth. For a nation is
    come up upon my land, strong, and without number;
    his teeth are the teeth of a lion, and he hath the
7 jaw teeth of a great lion. He hath laid my vine
    waste, and barked my fig tree: he hath made it
    clean bare, and cast it away; the branches thereof
8 are made white. Lament like a virgin girded with
9 sackcloth for the husband of her youth. The meal
    offering and the drink offering is cut off from the house
    of the LORD; the priests, the LORD's ministers, mourn.

---

6. a nation. For the question whether this term is to
be understood literally or figuratively see Introduction
pp. 4 ff.

8. In this verse the land or community is addressed.
The idea of the closest intimacy, symbolized by marriage,
between Jehovah and His people underlies this figure
which is very popular with O.T. prophets. Sacrifices
are the outward tokens of this fellowship. When the
sacrifices are interrupted, fellowship with God seems
interrupted, and the prophet compares the condition of
the community with that of a young widow.

sackcloth. This was the usual sign of mourning and
humiliation.

9. The meal offering. The *minchah* (which is here translated 'meal offering') is used (*a*) in the sense of a com-
plimentary gift to a man, i.e. in order to secure or retain
good-will; (*b*) in the sense of an offering made to God; and
(*c*) in the technical sense of a 'meal offering' as described
in Lev. ii. In some passages it is not clear whether the
reference is to (*b*) or (*c*). According to Exod. xxix. 38–42,
Numb. xxviii. 3–8 the meal offering and the drink offering
were to be offered twice daily, once with the morning burnt
offering and once with the evening burnt offering. See for
further information W. E. Barnes, *Companion to Biblical
Studies*, chap. XVI.

the drink offering. With the exception of Gen. xxxv. 14
the term is used in the technical sense of a definitely
prescribed offering of liquid.

The field is wasted, the land mourneth; for the corn 10
is wasted, the new wine is dried up, the oil languisheth.
Be ashamed, O ye husbandmen, howl, O ye vine- 11
dressers, for the wheat and for the barley; for the
harvest of the field is perished.   The vine is withered, 12
and the fig tree languisheth; the pomegranate tree,
the palm tree also, and the apple tree, even all the
trees of the field are withered: for joy is withered
away from the sons of men. Gird yourselves *with* 13
sackcloth, and lament, ye priests; howl, ye ministers
of the altar; come, lie all night in sackcloth, ye
ministers of my God: for the meal offering and the
drink offering is withholden from the house of your
God.

14–15. *A call to penitence and prayer.*

Sanctify a fast, call a solemn assembly, gather the 14

---

10. the land mourneth. This personification is a
favourite one with the prophets (see Hos. iv. 3; Amos i. 2;
Is. xxiv. 4; Jer. iv. 28; cf. Rom. viii. 22).

corn...new wine...oil. These are the three chief products of Palestine. The words used here may denote
either the products in their natural condition (viz. the
ears of corn, the juice of the grapes and the olives respectively) or as prepared and adapted for use.

is dried up. Read, with margin, 'is ashamed.' The
personification is continued. So also in *v*. 12.

12. The condition of things described in this verse
seems to be the result of a drought (cf. *vv*. 19, 20), not of
the locust-plague.

joy. Joy is especially connected with the harvest in the
O.T., see Is. ix. 3.

14. Sanctify a fast. Fasting in times of calamity is
mentioned on several occasions in the O.T. as practised
by the community as well as by individuals. The Day
of Atonement, instituted after the exile, was the one obli-
gatory fast in the year (Lev. xvi. 29, 31, xxiii. 27–32).
Four other fasts were added as memorials of days of
national calamity (see Zech. vii. 5, viii. 19). 1 Sam. xxxi. 13
shews that the practice was intended as a sign of mourning

old men *and* all the inhabitants of the land unto
the house of the LORD your God, and cry unto the
15 LORD.   Alas for the day! for the day of the LORD
is at hand, and as destruction from the Almighty shall
it come.

and grief. Its object was evidently to deprecate God's
wrath and win His compassion.

a solemn assembly.   The term which is here used in
a general sense was specially applied to the 7th day of the
Feast of Mazzoth or Unleavened Bread (Deut. xvi. 8) and
to the 8th day of the Feast of Tabernacles (Lev. xxiii. 36).
By later Jews the term was applied also to the Feast of
Weeks; see Jos. *Ant.* iii. x. 6.

15.   the day of the Lord: i.e. Jehovah. This expression is
frequent in the prophetical writings. It is apparently based
on a popular idea, already current in the days of Amos,
the earliest of our written prophecies, that Jehovah
would signally manifest Himself in triumph over Israel's
foes (see Amos v. 18). In adopting the phrase Amos
corrected the misconception by shewing that the Day of
Jehovah will be a Day in which His Righteousness will
be vindicated against *sin*, whether found in Israel or
amongst Israel's foes. It is the day in which God's
Honour will be vindicated, and those who share in His
Victory will be allowed to do so on the score of moral
character and not merely of privilege. From this thought
was developed the idea of judgement. Consequently
Isaiah and Zephaniah use the expression in connexion
with God's punishment of Israel by means of Assyria
and Babylon respectively. Jeremiah and Ezekiel use it of
the punishment in store for Egypt; and Joel, Zechariah,
and Malachi to denote the coming manifestation of the
Righteousness of Jehovah on a still larger scale. In this
larger sense it passed over into the New Testament and is
used by St Paul in his earliest epistle (1 Thessalonians)
and by other N.T. writers. Corresponding expressions
are found in the Gospels and other N.T. writings.

the day of the Lord...shall it come.   These words occur
verbatim in Is. xiii. 6 and were perhaps proverbial. In
the original Hebrew there is a play on the words 'destruction' (shōdh) and 'Almighty' (Shaddai). The exact meaning
of the Hebrew word, here translated 'Almighty,' is uncertain. The LXX translates it variously; in 15 places by
παντοκράτωρ, a word which describes the dominion of God

16–20. *The appalling condition of the country.*

Is not the meat cut off before our eyes, *yea,* 16
joy and gladness from the house of our God? The 17
seeds rot under their clods; the garners are laid
desolate, the barns are broken down; for the corn is
withered. How do the beasts groan! the herds of 18
cattle are perplexed, because they have no pasture;
yea, the flocks of sheep are made desolate. O LORD, 19
to thee do I cry: for the fire hath devoured the pastures of the wilderness, and the flame hath burned

---

over all that He has made as 'actually exercised' rather
than the abstract idea of God as 'being able to do all
things'; 'All-sovereign' rather than 'Almighty.'

16–18. These verses may be part of the prayer,
addressed to Jehovah in verses 19 and 20.

16. the meat. Rather, the food.

before our eyes. The nation was helpless, and unable
to avert the calamity, cf. Deut. xxviii. 31; Is. i. 7; Ps.
xxiii. 5.

joy and gladness...God. There can be no daily sacrifices,
no harvest festivals.

17. The seeds rot under their clods. Or perhaps 'The
grains shrivel under their shovels (or hoes),' i.e. on account
of the scorching heat. The LXX translates 'The kine are
unmanageable (?) in their stalls.' It is thought by some
that the words are hopelessly corrupt and that 17*b* is a
correction.

18. How do the beasts groan! The LXX connects
these words with *v.* 17 and translates 'What shall we lay
up in them?'

yea, the flocks of sheep. Rather, even the flocks of
sheep. Sheep are said to prefer the dry pastures of the
steppe.

are made desolate. This is the translation of the LXX.
The Hebrew word means 'to suffer punishment as a result
of guilt.' (As R.V. margin.) There may be a confusion
between two similar words in the Hebrew.

19. the fire. Possibly conflagrations kindled during
a drought, or the idea may be a figurative one.

the wilderness. That is uncultivated land, not sandy
desert.

20 all the trees of the field. Yea, the beasts of the field pant unto thee: for the water brooks are dried up, and the fire hath devoured the pastures of the wilderness.

ii. 1–2. *The day of Jehovah.*

2 Blow ye the trumpet in Zion, and sound an alarm in my holy mountain; let all the inhabitants of the land tremble: for the day of the LORD cometh, for
2 it is nigh at hand; a day of darkness and gloominess, a day of clouds and thick darkness, as the dawn spread upon the mountains; a great people and a strong, there hath not been ever the like, neither shall be any more after them, even to the years of many generations.

---

20. water brooks: i.e. channels of waters. The LXX translation ἀφέσεις ὑδάτων is the technical expression which in Ptolemaic and Roman days was applied to the irrigation ditches in Egypt.

ii. 1. the trumpet. Rather, the horn. The *shōphār* (as it was called) was made of ram's horn. It is still used in modern synagogues. Originally the *shōphār* was used for such purposes as giving signals in war, or raising an alarm, or announcing an accession. Another trumpet was the *chăẓōẓĕrāh*. This was a metal instrument, nearly a yard long, a straight slender tube having a slight expansion at the mouth with a bell-shaped end. It is depicted on the Arch of Titus. This clarion was chiefly used on religious occasions.

2. a day of darkness and gloominess...thick darkness. The same expression occurs in Zeph. i. 15, and the latter part of it in Ezek. xxxiv. 12, cf. Ezek. xxx. 3. There seems to be an allusion to the swarms of locusts.

as the dawn spread upon the mountains. The sun's rays reflected from the wings of the locusts would suggest this idea. Abrupt changes of metaphor are frequent in the prophets.

a great people and a strong. This phrase seems to be here used figuratively of the locusts; cf. i. 6, ii. 5, 11, 25.

there hath not been ever the like...: i.e. unprecedented; cf. Ex. x. 14.

3–11. *The attack of the locusts.*

A fire devoureth before them; and behind them a 3
flame burneth: the land is as the garden of Eden
before them, and behind them a desolate wilderness;
yea, and none hath escaped them. The appearance 4
of them is as the appearance of horses; and as
horsemen, so do they run. Like the noise of chariots 5
on the tops of the mountains do they leap, like
the noise of a flame of fire that devoureth the
stubble, as a strong people set in battle array. At 6
their presence the peoples are in anguish: all faces
are waxed pale. They run like mighty men; they 7
climb the wall like men of war; and they march
every one on his ways, and they break not their ranks.
Neither doth one thrust another; they march every 8
one in his path: and they burst through the weapons,
and break not off *their course*. They leap upon the 9
city; they run upon the wall; they climb up into the
houses; they enter in at the windows like a thief.

---

3. This verse is not to be understood literally. The
prophet pictures a contrast by comparing with the richness
of Eden the richness of the country before the locust came,
and the devastation after their passage with the devastation of fire; cf. Ezek. xxxvi. 35 and xxxi. 9, 16, 18.

**4. The appearance of them is as the appearance of
horses:** i.e. the head of a locust is like the head of a horse,
cf. Rev. ix. 7. The speed and close array of both are probably also in the prophet's thought.

5. Cf. Rev. ix. 9. **they leap,** i.e. the locusts. The
sound of their feeding is like the crackling of fire.

6. The anguish is caused by the prospect of famine
which inevitably ensues.

all faces are waxed pale. The expression occurs again
in Nahum ii. 11 and its meaning is very uncertain.

7. They run like mighty men. Better, They charge
like warriors; cf. Prov. xxx. 27.

8. they burst through the weapons. Better, as margin,
'and when they fall around the weapons they &c.,' i.e. even
weapons cannot arrest their progress.

9. the windows. Windows in Palestine were appa-

10 The earth quaketh before them; the heavens tremble:
the sun and the moon are darkened, and the stars
11 withdraw their shining: and the LORD uttereth his
voice before his army; for his camp is very great;
for he is strong that executeth his word: for the day
of the LORD is great and very terrible; and who can
abide it?

12–14. *A call to penitence.*

12 Yet even now, saith the LORD, turn ye unto me
with all your heart, and with fasting, and with
13 weeping, and with mourning: and rend your heart,
and not your garments, and turn unto the LORD
your God: for he is gracious and full of compassion,
slow to anger, and plenteous in mercy, and repenteth

---

rently lattice work without glass. Recent excavations
however attest that glass for other purposes was in use in
Palestine at a very early date.

10. the heavens. The Hebrews regarded the sky as
a solid vault; cf. iii. 15.

11. uttereth his voice: i.e. in thunder

his army: i.e. the locusts, see *v.* 25.

the day of the Lord. See note on i. 15.

12–14. A call to penitence.

12. saith the Lord. Literally, It is Jehovah's Oracle
(or Whisper). The expression is found very frequently in
all the prophets with the exception of Habakkuk and
Jonah, and is their regular formula in citing the divine
word. It is a solemn interjection almost restricted to the
prophetical writings, and probably denotes an intuition
which quietly arises in the prophet's mind and was regarded as a whispered revelation of Jehovah Himself.

. heart. In Hebrew the word translated 'heart' has
a very wide connotation. It includes mind and will. In
Hebrew psychology the 'heart' was regarded as the seat
of the intellect and will, not of the affections. Full moral
effort therefore is enjoined here.

13. rend your heart, and not your garments. Mere
external signs of penitence are insufficient without sincere
sorrow and full purpose of amendment; see Matt. vi. 16–18.

**gracious and full of compassion, slow to anger, and
plenteous in mercy.** This most wonderful description of
Jehovah's attitude towards the sinner was revealed to

him of the evil.　Who knoweth whether he will not 14
turn and repent, and leave a blessing behind him,
even a meal offering and a drink offering unto the
LORD your God?

15–17.　*A great penitential assembly.*

Blow the trumpet in Zion, sanctify a fast, call a 15
solemn assembly; gather the people, sanctify the 16
congregation, assemble the old men, gather the children, and those that suck the breasts: let the bridegroom go forth of his chamber, and the bride out of
her closet.　Let the priests, the ministers of the LORD, 17
weep between the porch and the altar, and let them

Moses on the Mount at the giving of the covenant laws
(see Ex. xxxiv. 6).　It made a great impression on the
best spirits in Israel as is shewn by their quotation no
less than a dozen times, especially in the Psalms (see Pss.
lxxxvi. 15, ciii. 8, cxi. 4, cxii. 4, cxlv. 8; Num. xiv. 18;
Neh. ix. 17, 31; 2 Chron. xxx. 9; Jer. xxxii. 18; Nah.
i. 3; Jon. iv. 2).　It seems probable that Exod. xx. 5, 6
(an explanatory comment on the second commandment)
was based on these words of Ex. xxxiv. 6.　The description
has been truly characterised as 'unsurpassed in literature.'

14.　Who knoweth whether he will not turn: viz. from
His intention of judgement.

a blessing.　The blessing consists in the restoration of
the fruits of the earth, and so the meal offering and the
drink offering can be restored.

15–17.　A great penitential assembly.

15.　the trumpet.　See note on ii. 1.

sanctify a fast.　See note on i. 14.

call a solemn assembly.　See note on i. 14.

16.　let the bridegroom...the bride.　Exemption from
military service and public duties was usually granted
to the newly-married (see Deut. xxiv. 5).　None, however,
were to be exempted from taking part in this great act of
penitence.　Its importance relegated all other obligations
to a secondary position.

closet.　A special nuptial tent is mentioned in 2 Sam. xvi. 22.

17.　the porch.　In 1 Kings vi. 3 the porch is mentioned
as being at the east end of the Temple.　In front of the
porch, the altar stood (see 1 Kings viii. 64).　This was in
'the court of the priests' (2 Chron. iv. 9) or 'the inner

say, Spare thy people, O LORD, and give not thine
heritage to reproach, that the nations should rule
over them : wherefore should they say among the
peoples, Where is their God ?

18-27.   *Jehovah's pity and promise of restoration.*

18   Then was the LORD jealous for his land, and had
19 pity on his people.   And the LORD answered and said
unto his people, Behold, I will send you corn, and
wine, and oil, and ye shall be satisfied therewith :
and I will no more make you a reproach among
20 the nations : but I will remove far off from you the
northern *army*, and will drive him into a land barren
and desolate, his forepart into the eastern sea, and
his hinder part into the western sea ; and his stink

---

court' (1 Kings vi. 36).   The same site is referred to in
Ezekiel viii. 16.

should rule over them.   Or, as margin, 'make proverbs
of them.'

18 ff.   Jehovah's answer and promises.

18.   jealous.   The relation between Jehovah and Israel is
often in the O.T. represented under the figure of marriage
(cf. i. 8), and probably this is the idea from which the phrase
was borrowed.   Hence Jehovah cannot endure the thought of
His people's dishonour.   As the word 'jealousy' is now used
chiefly in an evil sense, it seems strange and bold to modern
ears ; cf. the second commandment and 2 Cor. xi. 2.

19.   answer.   Probably Jehovah's answer came through
the prophet.

corn, and wine, and oil.   See note on i. 10.

20.   the northern army.   Literally, 'the northerner.'
The reference seems to be to the locust-swarm, although
locusts generally invade Palestine from the south or south-
east.   In Jeremiah the 'north' is constantly spoken of as
the quarter whence evil or invasion arises.   By his day
the term may have become a synonym for evil.

eastern...western sea : i.e. the Dead Sea and the Mediterranean.

his stink...his ill savour : i.e. the smell of the decaying
carcases of the locusts.

because he hath done great things : i.e. because the
locusts have acted arrogantly.   The fanciful ascription of

shall come up, and his ill savour shall come up,
because he hath done great things. Fear not, O land, 21
be glad and rejoice; for the LORD hath done great
things. Be not afraid, ye beasts of the field; for the 22
pastures of the wilderness do spring, for the tree
beareth her fruit, the fig tree and the vine do yield
their strength. Be glad then, ye children of Zion, 23
and rejoice in the LORD your God: for he giveth you
the former rain in just measure, and he causeth to
come down for you the rain, the former rain and the
latter rain, in the first *month*. And the floors shall 24

---

rational qualities to insects—and even to trees, mountains,
etc.—is common in O.T. prophets and psalmists (cf. Is.
xxxv. 1, xliv. 23, lv. 12; Ps. lxxxix. 12, xcviii. 8).

21–24. These verses interrupt Jehovah's answer. In
them the prophet speaks in his own words.

21. the Lord hath done great things. By a well-known
Hebrew usage called the 'prophetic perfect' the reference is
to the future; 'Jehovah will undoubtedly do great things.'

23. the former rain. This was called 'môreh' or
'yôreh.' It fell in October and November, the beginning
of the wet season in Palestine.

in just measure. Rather, as margin, 'according to His
righteousness.' Or it may mean 'as a token of your
restoration,' or 'for prosperity' (cf. Prov. viii. 18). It is
doubtful, however, if the word occurs in the O.T. in any
other than a moral sense. The Vulgate, following an old
Jewish interpretation, translates 'he giveth you a teacher
of righteousness' (cf. A.V. margin), and moderns who adopt
this rendering see in it a Messianic reference.

the latter rain. This was called 'malqôsh.' It was the
spring rain which matured the crops. It fell in March
and April and closed the wet season.

the first month. The italics shew that 'month' is an
interpretation. The margin reads 'at the first,' drawing
a contrast between the material blessings and the spiritual
blessings which are to come 'afterward' (see *v*. 28). The
LXX and Vulgate seem to have understood the phrase to
mean 'as aforetime.' It is true that Nisan, the first month
of the ecclesiastical year, would synchronize with the
period of 'the spring rain.'

24. the floors: i.e. the threshing-floors. The threshing-

be full of wheat, and the fats shall overflow with wine
25 and oil.   And I will restore to you the years that the
locust hath eaten, the cankerworm, and the caterpiller,
and the palmerworm, my great army which I sent
26 among you.   And ye shall eat in plenty and be
satisfied, and shall praise the name of the LORD your
God, that hath dealt wondrously with you : and my
27 people shall never be ashamed.   And ye shall know
that I am in the midst of Israel, and that I am the
LORD your God, and there is none else : and my
people shall never be ashamed.

28–29.   *The outpouring of Jehovah's Spirit.*

28   And it shall come to pass afterward, that I will
pour out my spirit upon all flesh ; and your sons and

---

floor was a circular piece of ground, in the centre of which
was piled in a heap the ears and stalks of corn.   In threshing, the ears and stalks were laid out and a threshing board
drawn over them.   After this process the grain was win-
nowed with a fan or by the wind.

the fats.   Rather, 'the (wine) vats.'   These vats were
troughs or hollows excavated in the rock.   They received
the juice which was trodden out in the winepress.

25.   I : i.e. Jehovah.

my great army.   The LXX translation is 'my great
Power.'   The Arians, interpreting the words to denote God's
Son, argued from this verse that 'the Son is the Power of
God in no higher sense than any other agency by which great
effects are wrought upon the face of nature' (Swete).

27.   And ye shall know that...I am the Lord.   This is
a stereotyped phrase in the O.T., very frequent especially
in Ezekiel.   It occurs chiefly in connexion with announce-
ments or descriptions of God's judgements.

28–29.   The outpouring of the Spirit.

28.   my spirit.   The Spirit of God in the O.T. is that by
which God creates and sustains the life of His creatures
(Gen. i. 2).   It inspired the ecstatic state of prophecy.   It
impelled the prophets to teach and warn; and imparted
warlike energy to heroes, such as the judges and kings in
ancient Israel.   It also imparted executive and adminis-
trative power to the Messianic King (Is. xi. 2) and to the

your daughters shall prophesy, your old men shall
dream dreams, your young men shall see visions:
and also upon the servants and upon the handmaids 29
in those days will I pour out my spirit.

30–31. *The signs of the great and terrible day of Jehovah.*

And I will shew wonders in the heavens and in the 30
earth, blood, and fire, and pillars of smoke. The sun 31
shall be turned into darkness, and the moon into

'Servant of Jehovah' (Is. xlii. 1). Technical skill was
attributed to the Spirit of God (Ex. xxxi. 3). 'The angel
of the Presence' is in Is. lxiii. 9–11 identified with His
holy Spirit. Haggai and Zechariah think of the Spirit
of the Lord of hosts as standing in the midst of the people
and fulfilling God's promises. And in Ps. cxxxix. 7 the
Spirit of Jehovah is identified with the omnipresent God.
It remained for the Personality of the Holy Spirit to be
revealed in N.T. days. St Peter sees a fulfilment of the
prophecy in the present verse on the Day of Pentecost
(see Acts ii. 17–21). In this connexion it is interesting
to notice the wish of Moses in the day that the Spirit of
Jehovah rested upon the elders of Israel (see Num. xi. 29).
Ezekiel and Jeremiah also taught that the gift of the
Spirit is universal (see Ezek. xxxvi. 27; Jer. xxxi. 33, 34),
a truth in which St Paul glories (Eph. iv. 3, 4; 1 Cor. xii.
4–11).

all flesh. Although this expression is used in the O.T.
(e.g. Is. xl. 5, xlix. 26) of all mankind, here it may refer
to Israel only.

prophesy. In its earliest forms prophecy was a sort of
religious ecstasy often produced with the aid of music
(see 1 Sam. x. 5); but in later days it was calm inspired
instruction in moral and religious truth. Prediction was
sometimes an element. It was not however essential.
Some think that the reference here is to an ecstatic spiritual
state, and they would explain it as equivalent to 'speak
with tongues.' Accordingly they see no allusion to a moral
transformation nor spiritual renewal nor deeper insight
into Divine truth.

young men. The original word denotes those in the
prime of manhood.

30–31. wonders. They serve to display God's power.

31. the moon into blood. This is apocalyptic imagery,

blood, before the great and terrible day of the LORD
come.

32. *The escape of the remnant.*

32 And it shall come to pass, that whosoever shall call
on the name of the LORD shall be delivered: for in
mount Zion and in Jerusalem there shall be those
that escape, as the LORD hath said, and among the
remnant those whom the LORD doth call.

iii. 1–8. *Jehovah's judgement of all nations in the valley
of Jehoshaphat.*

3 For, behold, in those days, and in that time, when
I shall bring again the captivity of Judah and Jeru-
2 salem, I will gather all nations, and will bring

---

probably to denote the decay and collapse of society. It
may have been suggested by eclipses or by atmospheric
disturbances.

before the great and terrible day of the Lord come.
The words occur verbatim in Mal. iv. 5, see note on
i. 15.

32.   call on the name of the Lord : i.e. genuinely invoke
Jehovah's gracious help.   These words are quoted in
Rom. x. 13.

in mount Zion...escape.   These words occur verbatim
Obad. 17 and the words 'as the Lord hath said' support
the idea that the expression is quoted from Obadiah.

the remnant. Better, 'the survivors.'   The LXX has
an interesting variant here. Instead of 'survivors' it
reads 'those who are bearing good tidings.' *vv.* 28–32 are
quoted in Acts ii. 17–21; cf. also *v.* 39.

iii. G. A. Smith thinks that this chapter 'was delivered
by Joel at another time and in different circumstances
from the rest of his prophecies.'   He sees no connexion
with the foregoing.

1. I shall bring again the captivity. This rendering
of the Hebrew is by no means certain. The words may
equally well be rendered 'I shall turn the fortune' (cf.
Job xlii. 10). This latter rendering contains no inherent
reference to a 'captivity' and consequently the phrase
cannot be pressed in the interests of a pre-exilic date.

them down into the valley of Jehoshaphat; and
I will plead with them there for my people and
for my heritage Israel, whom they have scattered
among the nations, and parted my land. And they 3
have cast lots for my people: and have given a boy
for an harlot, and sold a girl for wine, that they might
drink. Yea, and what are ye to me, O Tyre, and 4
Zidon, and all the regions of Philistia? will ye render
me a recompence? and if ye recompense me, swiftly

---

2. the valley of Jehoshaphat. The valley, or rather
dale, of Jehoshaphat occurs again in *v.* 12. Six persons
bearing the name Jehoshaphat are mentioned in the O.T.
including a king of Judah. The name means 'Jehovah
hath judged' (see R.V. marg. on *v.* 12) and it seems to
be the symbolical import of the name which has determined
its selection by the prophet as representing the scene of
ultimate judgement. The name may be purely an imaginary
one. Those who do not accept this view have identified it
with (i) the scene of the battle recounted in 2 Chron. xx.
20–24; or with (ii) the present 'Valley of Jehoshaphat'
which is identical with the Wâdy of the Kidron of 2 Sam.
xv. 23. The Koran has a description of a 'day of the
Lord' which bears a close resemblance to that described
here; and according to Col. Sir Chas. Warren, on a column
which juts out from the east wall overhanging the Wâdy of
the Kidron devout Moslems in the early morning practise
the first step into paradise.

3. cast lots. The same expression occurs verbatim in
Nah. iii. 10; Obad. 11. In ancient warfare it was the
custom for the conquerors to divide amongst themselves
the captives by lot (cf. Judges v. 30).

a boy for an harlot. 'For' = 'in exchange for' or 'as
the price of.'

4. what are ye to me. These words may mean
(*a*) 'what have ye to do with me?' (as A.V.), or (*b*) what
would ye do to me? i.e. will ye repay me? or (*c*) what do
you want of me?

will ye render me...recompense me. Better, as margin,
Will ye repay a deed of mine, or will ye do aught unto
me? i.e. Have I (through Israel) done you any wrong, or
is it an unprovoked attack on me (as Israel's God)? The
defeat of a nation was regarded as the defeat of its god.

and speedily will I return your recompence upon your
5 own head.   Forasmuch as ye have taken my silver
and my gold, and have carried into your temples my
6 goodly pleasant things; the children also of Judah
and the children of Jerusalem have ye sold unto the
sons of the Grecians, that ye might remove them far
7 from their border: behold, I will stir them up out of
the place whither ye have sold them, and will return
8 your recompence upon your own head; and I will
sell your sons and your daughters into the hand of
the children of Judah, and they shall sell them to
the men of Sheba, to a nation far off: for the LORD
hath spoken it.

9–17.   *Multitudes in the valley of decision.*
9   Proclaim ye this among the nations; prepare war:

Hence the point of this question.   Jehovah will vindicate
His honour (*vv.* 4, 7) by giving Judah victory (*v.* 8).

will I return your recompence upon your own head. The
expression occurs again in Obad. 15; cf. Ps. vii. 17.

5.   temples.   Or, palaces, i.e. houses of the wealthy.

my goodly pleasant things: valuable treasures.

6.   The reference is to slave-dealing.

sons of the Grecians.   The Hebrew word bears a resemblance to the original Greek term for the Ionians.   The
trade between Tyre and Ionia is referred to in Ezek. xxvii.
13.   The reference may be to the Ionians of Asia Minor.

8.   This is an instance of the *lex talionis*, the law of
requital.

the men of Sheba.   The Sabaeans dwelt in south-west
Arabia.   A Sabaean Queen visited Solomon (see 1 Kings
x. 1–13).   Many references are found in the prophetical
writings and one in the Psalms (lxxii. 15) to their exports.
Certain Sabaean inscriptions have been discovered to-
gether with considerable finds of Sabaean coins.   The
Sabaean State existed till the sixth century of our era.
Instead of 'Sabaeans' the LXX here reads 'into captivity.'

to a nation far off.   Bewer would translate 'for a nation
far off' and regard the Sabaeans as middlemen; but cf.
Gen. xxxvii. 36.

9.   prepare war.   The original word means 'sanctify'

stir up the mighty men; let all the men of war draw
near, let them come up. Beat your plowshares into 10
swords, and your pruninghooks into spears: let the
weak say, I am strong. Haste ye, and come, all ye 11
nations round about, and gather yourselves together:
thither cause thy mighty ones to come down, O LORD.
Let the nations bestir themselves, and come up to 12
the valley of Jehoshaphat: for there will I sit to
judge all the nations round about. Put ye in the 13
sickle, for the harvest is ripe: come, tread ye; for
the winepress is full, the fats overflow; for their
wickedness is great. Multitudes, multitudes in the 14
valley of decision! for the day of the LORD is near

---

or 'consecrate' (see margin).   Before a campaign sacrifices
were offered (see Jer. vi. 4; Mic. iii. 5; 1 Sam. vii. 8, 9).

10. Beat your plowshares into swords. The opposite
process is mentioned in Is. ii. 4 (and Mic. iv. 3).

11. Haste ye. The meaning of the Hebrew word is
uncertain.

thy mighty ones. Probably the reference is to the
angelic host. Apparently the LXX understood the last
part of the verse to mean 'Let the peaceful one be a
warrior' (cf. *v.* 10).

12. the valley of Jehoshaphat. See note on *v.* 2. *vv.* 12
and 13 seem to be Jehovah's reply.

13. Put ye in the sickle. Probably a small instrument
for cutting grapes is meant. Bewer translates 'Apply
the pruning knives'; cf. Rev. xiv. 15 for the figure.

the harvest is ripe. If Bewer's translation (see previous
note) is correct, the translation here will be 'the vintage is
ripe' (as the margin reads).

come: i.e. into the winepress.

tread ye. This is the LXX rendering. The meaning
'get you down' (sc. into the winepress in order to tread)
is well established for the Hebrew original but the meaning
'tread' is doubtful.

the fats. See note on ii. 24.

14. multitudes. The Hebrew word is very expressive.
It connotes the confused noise made by a crowd of people.
LXX renders 'noises sounded forth.'

the day of the Lord. See note on i. 15.

15 in the valley of decision. The sun and the moon are
16 darkened, and the stars withdraw their shining. And
the LORD shall roar from Zion, and utter his voice
from Jerusalem; and the heavens and the earth shall
shake: but the LORD will be a refuge unto his people,
17 and a strong hold to the children of Israel. So shall
ye know that I am the LORD your God, dwelling in
Zion my holy mountain: then shall Jerusalem be
holy, and there shall no strangers pass through
her any more.

18–20. *Judah's everlasting prosperity.*

18 And it shall come to pass in that day, that the
mountains shall drop down sweet wine, and the
hills shall flow with milk, and all the brooks of
Judah shall flow with waters; and a fountain shall
come forth of the house of the LORD, and shall water
19 the valley of Shittim. Egypt shall be a desolation,

---

15. The same words are found in ii. 10.
16. the Lord shall roar...Jerusalem. The same expression occurs verbatim in Amos i. 2.
18. the mountains shall drop down sweet wine. An exaggerated expression used apparently to convey the idea of great fertility. See Amos ix. 13.
a fountain. Ezekiel in his 47th chapter describes a stream that issued from the Temple and fertilized the desert, sweetening the waters of the Dead Sea. Isaiah in his 8th chapter had already seen in the waters of Siloah a symbol of Jehovah's silent, unobtrusive and life-giving presence; cf. Zech. xiv. 8. Fertility was regarded in ancient belief as indicating the dwelling-place of a deity.
the valley of Shittim. Shittim means 'acacias' (cf. margin). The fact that acacias grow in dry soil gives the point to the statement. The identification of 'the gorge' (for such is the meaning of the Hebrew word) is uncertain.
It has been identified with Abel-shittim of Num. xxxiii. 49. It is more likely to be the valley of Kidron on the east of Jerusalem (see G. A. Smith, *Jerusalem*, Vol. 1.

and Edom shall be a desolate wilderness, for the
violence done to the children of Judah, because they
have shed innocent blood in their land.   But Judah 20
shall abide for ever, and Jerusalem from generation
to generation.   And I will cleanse their blood that 21
I have not cleansed: for the LORD dwelleth in Zion.

---

plates IV and V) or the Wâdy es-Sant (probably the vale
of Elah, 1 Sam. xviii. 2-19, xxi. 9) which is in the
Shephelah some miles south-west of Jerusalem (see
G. A. Smith's *Historical Geography*, plate IV).

19. The contrast with Judah's typical foes not only
heightens the effect of the blessedness of Judah; it
vindicates Judah's honour (see *v.* 21).

innocent blood. This seems to imply an unprovoked
massacre of the Jews.

20. abide. Better 'be inhabited' (as margin).   Hence
it will always flourish.

21. cleanse. Better 'hold as innocent' (as margin).
By making Egypt and Edom desolate, Jehovah will shew
in an unmistakable manner that the massacre inflicted
on them by these peoples was unprovoked.   LXX
apparently reads 'I will avenge.'

THE
BOOK OF OBADIAH

INTRODUCTION

§ 1. THE PROPHET OBADIAH.

Obadiah is a name borne by many persons in the
Old Testament history. It was the name of a man who
was apparently the Royal Chamberlain or governor of
Ahab's palace (1 Kings xviii.). In the reign of King
Jehoshaphat of Judah a man named Obadiah, who is
called a prince, was sent to teach the law to the people
throughout all the cities of Judah (2 Chron. xvii. 7).
Later, in the days of Josiah, a man named Obadiah was
appointed one of the overseers of the workmen who
repaired the Temple. He was a Levite of the sons of
Merari (2 Chron. xxxiv. 12). In addition to these the
name is frequently found in the genealogical lists contained in the first book of Chronicles (cc. iii., vii., viii.,
ix.) and in the list of the rulers of the tribes of Israel in
1 Chron. xxvii. After the Babylonian exile the name
reappears in the list of those Heads of the Fathers'
Houses who went up with Ezra to Jerusalem (Ezra
viii.). In Neh. x. an Obadiah is mentioned amongst
those who with Nehemiah sealed the covenant. He
was a priest. In Neh. xii. 25 a levitical chief named
Obadiah is mentioned, who was appointed as a singer
in the Temple. Unless the prophet Obadiah is to be
identified with any of these, we know nothing about
him except what may be gathered from the prophecy;
and from this we gather that he was a native of Judah.

The name may mean either 'servant of Yah' or 'worshipper of Yah.' The former part of the name occurs very frequently in proper names not only in the O.T. but in Phoenician, Palmyrene, Aramaean and Arabian proper names. It appears under varying forms, such as Obed, Obod, Ebed, Abed, Abda, Abd, Abdi. It may be simply a title of an office, as the name Malachi apparently was (see p. 87), but in the present case this is unlikely. The latter part of the name is also found very frequently in proper names (e.g. Isaiah, Jeremiah, Elijah, etc.).

'Yah' alone as the name of Israel's God occurs in Ex. xv. 2, xvii. 16; Is. xxvi. 4, xxxviii. 11; Song of Songs viii. 6; and many times in the late Psalms, especially in the exclamation 'Halleluyah' which means 'Praise ye Yah.' It is a poetical abbreviation of Yahweh, and is the Divine Name as revealed to Moses (see Ex. iii. 14). Although the name Yahweh was probably not new to Moses or the Israelites, it expressed the infinite possibilities of the Divine Character as it would manifest itself progressively under the varying circumstances of national life. In the English Bible it appears in some passages under the form 'Jehovah.' Whatever may have been the original pronunciation of the name, it is certain that it was not Jehovah. In consequence of Ex. xx. 7 the Jews for a long time considered that the Divine Name was too sacred to be uttered. So the original pronunciation is now a matter of conjecture. 'Jehovah' is a blending of the original consonants with the vowels of the Hebrew word for 'Lord,' and, so far as is known, was not introduced into modern speech before the 15th or 16th century of our era. The usage of the Revised Version of the English Bible in regard to the word 'Jehovah' is stated in the fourth paragraph of the

Preface to the O.T. of this version. 'Yahweh' was probably the original pronunciation, and it is to be hoped that in time it will be universally adopted, or some equivalent which will clearly express its meaning, such as the Self-Revealer.

If the present book contains within it an earlier prophecy (see § 2), it remains uncertain whether Obadiah was the author of the earlier prophecy, or was the name of one of the editors who incorporated the earlier prophecy in the present book. Of course the name may have been borne both by the earlier prophet and one of his editors, but this is improbable.

§ 2. THE UNITY OF THE PROPHECY.

The relation of the prophecy of Obadiah to Jeremiah xlix. presents a problem to which different answers have been given. Verses occur in both chapters which are almost word for word the same, and cannot be independent of one another.

OBADIAH 1—4.

We have heard tidings from the Lord, and an ambassador is sent among the nations, saying, Arise ye, and let us rise up against her in battle. Behold, I have made thee small among the nations: thou art greatly despised. The pride of thine heart hath deceived thee, O thou that dwellest in the clefts of the rock, whose habitation is high; that saith in his heart, Who shall bring me down to the ground? Though thou mount on high as the eagle, and though thy nest be set among the stars, I will bring thee down from thence, saith the Lord.

JEREMIAH XLIX. 14—16.

I have heard tidings from the Lord, and an ambassador is sent among the nations, saying, Gather yourselves together, and come against her, and rise up to the battle. For, behold, I have made thee small among the nations, and despised among men. As for thy terribleness, the pride of thine heart hath deceived thee, O thou that dwellest in the clefts of the rock, that holdest the height of the hill: though thou shouldest make thy nest as high as the eagle, I will bring thee down from thence, saith the Lord.

OBADIAH 5, 6a.

If thieves came to thee, if robbers by night (how art thou cut off!) would they not steal till they had enough? if grape-gatherers came to thee, would they not leave some gleaning grapes? How are the things of Esau searched out!

JEREMIAH XLIX. 9—10a.

If grapegatherers came to thee, would they not leave some gleaning grapes? if thieves by night, would they not destroy till they had enough? I have made Esau bare.

Three explanations of the relation of these two passages immediately present themselves.

Either (1) the prophet Jeremiah has borrowed the passage from the book of Obadiah;

or (2) Obadiah has borrowed from Jeremiah's writings;

or (3) Jeremiah and Obadiah have both incorporated an earlier prophet's words into their own writings. Or possibly later editors of the writings of Jeremiah and Obadiah have done so.

In order to arrive at a decision our chief guides are the signs which the passages themselves offer.

On close examination of the passages it is clear that there are certain differences as well as resemblances. Each passage has additions which are not found in the other; and in a few cases individual words in both passages differ. From these indications it seems probable that an earlier prophecy has been incorporated with some modification and expansion into the prophecies of both Obadiah and Jeremiah either by these prophets themselves or by their editors. Compare a similar instance in Isaiah ii. 2—4 and Micah iv. 1—3.

This conclusion is not unanimously accepted. Explanations (1) and (2) have their advocates on grounds which, whilst they are not convincing, are plausible. Certainty is at present unattainable in the matter, nor does the lack of certainty in any way affect the teaching of the book, which after all is the most important consideration. The problem, however, involves the question of the date of Obadiah's prophecy and the mode of the compilation and transmission of O.T. prophecy and is interesting in that connexion.

There are further reasons for regarding the book as a compilation. When *vv.* 1—9 are compared with *vv.* 10—21, the following marked differences appear: (*a*) the style of the latter verses is diffuse. On the other hand *vv.* 1—9 are full of striking imagery and the style is concise and spirited. (*b*) Again, *vv.* 1—9 imply an overthrow of Edom by its allies which is already an event of *the past*. *Vv.* 10—21 point to a judgement which is to overtake Edom *in the future* along with other nations.

It seems probable therefore that the book embodies the writings of at least three different persons: (1) the author of the early prophecy embedded in *vv.* 1—9; (2) the author of *vv.* 1—9 who wrote after a signal overthrow of Edom by certain unnamed allies; and (3) the author of *vv.* 10—21 who wrote after a captivity of Jerusalem (see *v.* 20).

To what extent other hands have had a share in the compilation of this book is a matter of over-refined criticism and is of little or no profit to our present purpose.

§ 3. The Date of the Prophecy.

The question discussed in the previous section has a direct bearing on the date of the prophecy. It is quite clear that if Jeremiah quoted from Obadiah's prophecy, then Obadiah must have been earlier than or at least contemporary with Jeremiah. If on the other hand Obadiah borrowed from Jeremiah's writings then Obadiah must have been later than Jeremiah unless he was a contemporary. If, however, the conclusion arrived at above in § 2 is accepted, the date of Obadiah is left independent of the date of Jeremiah, and rests chiefly upon what may be inferred from the contents of the prophecy itself. Now verses 10—14 refer to a capture of Jerusalem in which Edom played a hostile part. So far as we know from the O.T. Scriptures Jerusalem was attacked on the following occasions:

(a) In the fifth year of Rehoboam when Shishak, King of Egypt, despoiled Solomon's temple and the royal palace of their treasures (1 Kings xiv. 25 f.).

(b) In 2 Chron. xx. 1—30 there is an account of a threatened attack by the children of Ammon, Moab, and Mount Seir on Jerusalem in the reign of Jehoshaphat. The invasion, however, came to nought for 'the children of Ammon and Moab stood up against the inhabitants of Mount Seir utterly to slay and destroy them' (v. 23).

(c) In the days of King Jehoram of Judah, when Philistines and Arabians invaded Judah and carried off much substance and many of Jehoram's sons and wives from his palace (2 Chron. xxi. 16 f.).

(d) In the reign of Amaziah when King Joash of Israel brake down the wall of Jerusalem from the gate of Ephraim unto the corner gate and the temple and the royal palace were stripped of their treasures (2 Kings xiv. 13 f.).

(e) About 734 B.C. Rezin, King of Syria, and Pekah, King of Israel, came up to Jerusalem to war, and they besieged King Ahaz, but could not overcome him (2 Kings xvi. 5).

(f) Again about 701 B.C. Sennacherib, King of Assyria, besieged Hezekiah in Jerusalem, but was finally compelled to withdraw without taking the city (2 Kings xviii., xix.).

(g) In 597 B.C. Jerusalem was taken and despoiled by Nebuchadrezzar, King of Babylon, and Jehoiachin, King of Judah, with others, was carried away captive to Babylon (2 Kings xxiv. 11—16).

(h) Then in 586 B.C. Jerusalem was again besieged by Nebuchadrezzar; King Zedekiah and the chief men were carried captive to Babylon. The city was razed to the ground and only the poorest were left behind under a governor Gedaliah (2 Kings xxv. 1—23).

Before we can associate *vv.* 10—14 with any of these occasions, we must enquire whether there are any records of the attitude of Edom towards Judah on these several occasions?

There seems to be none except in the cases of (*e*) and (*h*).

In 2 Chron. xxviii. 17 we are simply told that in the reign of Ahaz the Edomites came and smote Judah and carried away captives. When, however, Nebuchadrezzar destroyed Jerusalem in 586 B.C., Ezekiel (xxxv. 3—15) tells us that not only did Edom take an active part in the hostilities, she also 'rejoiced over the inheritance of the house of Israel, because it was desolate' (cf. also Lam. iv. 21, 22; Is. xxxiv., lxvi. 1—6; Psalm cxxxvii. 7). The hostility of the Edomites to Israel was of long standing (see Amos i. 11, 12; Joel iii. 19; Jer. xlix. 7–22; Ezek. xxv. 12—14; Mal. i. 3, 4) and found its fullest expression in 586 B.C. It can hardly be doubted then that the reference in *vv.* 10—14 of Obadiah's prophecy is to the sack of Jerusalem by Nebuchadrezzar in 586 B.C.

We must now turn to Obadiah 1—9 and ask what occasions are recorded when Edom was overthrown by its own allies. So far as the Bible record goes, there is only one occasion on which such a misfortune befell her. That is the occasion recounted in 2 Chron. xx. 1—30 and already referred to, when in a threatened attack on Jerusalem in the reign of Jehoshaphat 'the children of Ammon and Moab stood up against the inhabitants of Mount Seir utterly to slay and destroy them.'

It is possible that the early prophecy in Obad. 1—4, 5, 6a may refer to this occasion. But, when this is granted, the question remains, on what occasion did the later writer make use of it? 'All the men of thy confederacy have brought thee on thy way, even to the border: the men that were at peace with thee have deceived thee, and prevailed against thee; they that eat thy bread lay a snare under thee' (v. 7) seems hardly applicable to the Ammonites and Moabites; nor can the words with any confidence be applied either to the Assyrians or Babylonians. To whom can they apply? From early days Edom seems to have been closely allied with Arab tribes (cf. Gen. xxv. 13, xxxvi.). Little is known of the history of these tribes until the 4th century B.C. when we find Nabataeans, who were Arabians, settled in Petra the ancient capital of the Edomites (see Diod. XIX. 94—100). Ezekiel (xxv. 4, 5, 10) seems to refer to a great northward movement of Arabs in his day. The allusion in Mal. i. 3, 4 would seem to place the dispossession of Edom by the Nabataeans some time before the middle of the 5th century B.C. Obadiah 7 may then reasonably be regarded as referring to this expulsion of the Edomites from their country by the Nabataeans.

To sum up we may say that the book of Obadiah reached its present form about the middle of the 5th century B.C. The latest editor made use of prophecies to which earlier circumstances gave rise. One of those circumstances was almost certainly the capture of Jerusalem 586 B.C. and the other may have been the threatened attack on Jerusalem in the reign of Jehoshaphat. It cannot be now determined whether Obadiah was the name of the author of the early prophecy or of one or other of the post-exilic editors. It is of course possible, but hardly likely, that the name was borne by all three.

§ 4. EDOM AND ITS PEOPLE.

Edom was the name of a land which lay towards the south and south-east of Palestine. The derivation of the name is uncertain. The proper name Obed-Edom in 2 Sam. vi. creates a presumption that Edom was the name of a god. The Hebrew word for 'red' bears a close resemblance to the word Edom, and it is possible that the land was so-called from the red colour of its sandstone cliffs. Gen. xxv. 25, 30 allude to this derivation. Too much importance however may be attached to this and other biblical derivations of name. There is reason to believe that in this and like cases, the biblical writers were only indicating a resemblance between the sounds of two words, not an etymological connexion.

The land of Edom is also called by two other names in the Bible, namely Seir and Esau (see Gen. xxxii. 3, xxxvi. 1; Obad. 8). The name Seir is perhaps connected with the Hebrew word meaning 'hairy' and may allude to the shrubby or wooded character of the land. Esau also seems to mean 'hairy' (cf. Gen. xxv. 25). G. A. Smith compares the Phoenician mythical hunter *Usoos* and suggests that Esau may have been the name of a god.

The country consists of two mountain ranges with

a broad valley of 10 to 12 miles separating them. The whole territory is roughly a square some 125 miles in either direction, and is largely desert, although the Eastern Range—the Mt Esau of the O.T.—was well-watered from springs and afforded pasture for cattle and fodder for camels. Its importance was chiefly due to its geographical position, situated as it was between Egypt and Syria on the one hand and between Arabia and the Red Sea and the Mediterranean on the other.

Such a country was fitted to breed a sturdy and uncivilised people. And if the subsequent character of the people has been reflected back in Genesis into their ancestor Esau, the suggestion of G. A. Smith that a 'man of the field' in Gen. xxv. 27 implies a reversion to a less civilised form of society aptly describes their culture as never reaching beyond a low stage.

According to Deut. ii. 12 (cf. Gen. xiv. 6) Seir was aforetime the home of Horites, whom the Edomites dispossessed. The name Horite probably means a cave dweller. Many caves, hewn in the sandstone, are still to be seen and give point to the description in Obad. 3. Mr R. A. S. Macalister has recently excavated at Gezer the remains of cave-dwellers 'not much later than 3000 B.C.' There is, however, no evidence to connect them with the Horites. It seems probable that the Horites were not exterminated but mingled with the Edomites (see Gen. xxxvi.).

The Edomites are said to be the descendants of Esau, Jacob's brother. The names of the clans with their clan-chiefs are given in Gen. xxxvi. together with a list of the clans and clan-chiefs of the Horites. The names of eight kings of Edom before the days of Saul are also given. From this chapter it may be inferred that the Edomites occupied their territory before the entry of Israel into Canaan and that their

monarchy, which was not hereditary (cf. Is. xxxiv. 12),
was established before the Israelitish kingdom (cf.
Numbers xx. 14).

The contact of Israel with Edom from the earliest
days to the latest was one of bitter and unabated
hostility—an hostility to which not only the historical
books but also psalmists and prophets bear ample
testimony and which is deprecated in Deut. xxiii. 7
(cf. ii. 4, 5).

Edom refused to give Israel passage through its
territory as the latter journeyed on their way to the
promised land after the Exodus from Egypt (Numbers
xx. 14—21; Judges xi. 17, 18). Saul, Israel's first king,
warred with Edom and according to the LXX of
1 Sam. xiv. 17 was victorious. David also subdued
them and put garrisons throughout all Edom (2 Sam.
viii. 14). However, in Solomon's time they rose up
again under Hadad (1 Kings xi. 14) and maintained
their position sometimes as vassals to Judah (see
1 Kings xxii. 47; 2 Kings iii. 19), at other times,
especially between the reigns of Joram and Amaziah,
as an independent state (see 2 Kings viii. 20—22,
xiv. 7, 10; 2 Chr. xxi. 8—10, xxv. 14, 19). In the days
of Ahaz, Edom smote Judah and carried away captives (see 2 Chr. xxviii. 17, cf. 2 Kings xvi. 6). When
the Assyrians threatened the smaller states of the
west, Edom threw in her lot with her neighbours and
joined the league against Assyria. With them she
paid tribute to Tiglath-pileser and other Assyrian
kings. Ps. cxxxvii. 7 depicts the attitude of Edom
towards the Jews at the siege of Jerusalem by the
Babylonian king Nebuchadrezzar in 586 B.C. Shortly
after this time the Edomites occupied Southern Judah
and established themselves in Hebron (see Ezek. xxxv.
10 f., xxxvi. 5). This incursion was no doubt the result

of pressure on their southern and eastern borders by Nabataean Arabs. Driven before this northward invasion, they naturally swarmed into Southern Judah. From Hebron the Edomites were dislodged in the 2nd century B.C. by the Maccabaean heroes (see I Macc. v. 65; Jos. *Antiq.* XII. viii. 6). Finally John Hyrcanus conquered the Idumaeans (as the Edomites were now called) and compelled them to adopt Judaism (see Jos. *Antiq.* XIII. xi. 1). From this time the Idumaeans were incorporated with the Jews and it was from one of the Idumaean families that the dynasty of the Herods of N.T. times sprang. The memory of the fierce hostility between Israel and Edom survived amongst the Jews of the Middle Ages, for in the contemporary writings of Abarbanel, Rashi and Kimchi their persecutors of those later days are alluded to under the sobriquet of Edom and Bozrah.

§ 5. THE RELIGIOUS TEACHING OF THE PROPHECY.

No fact is more clearly marked in the pages of the O.T. than the bitter hatred which existed between Israel and Edom. From the day when the twin brothers Jacob and Esau wrestled in the womb of their mother—surely a significant omen—to the day of the Idumaean dynasty of the Herods the hostility pursued an almost unbroken course.

Various causes contributed to it. In the days of the kings Judah cast envious eyes on Edom's rich trade with Arabia and Phoenicia. The port of Elath with Ezion-Geber on the Gulf of Akaba was always a bone of contention; and commercial avarice explains the constant friction in the days of Solomon (I Kings ix. 26—28), Jehoshaphat (I Kings xxii. 47—48), Amaziah

(2 Kings xiv. 22, cf. *v.* 7) and Ahaz (2 Kings xvi. 6).
A reminiscence of this old sore is found in Obadiah 6.

Again, Edom was as different from Israel in temper-
ament and character as Esau was from Jacob. As
Esau despised his birthright, had no higher aspira-
tions than those which the visible order satisfied, gave
no thought to the demands of his spiritual nature, so
Edom, in spite of its worldly shrewdness (Obad. 8),
found ample security in its mountain fastnesses
(Obad. 3), and was deaf to the call of high ideals or
natural feelings (Obad. 10, 11), proud, isolated and
revengeful (Obad. 12). Israel, too, had her uninspired
days. Yet even in the darkest days a brilliant faith in
the Unseen God shone out. She knew how to dare and
to suffer for higher things than this world affords.
With an inextinguishable hope she kept the vision
ever in mind, and though it tarried, there were always
those in Israel who waited for it.

No doubt human passion found expression in
Israel's triumph at Edom's troubles and defeats. But
it was not unmixed with a higher element. The overthrow and defeat of ' the profane ' (cf. Heb. xii, 16) was
felt to be a necessary step towards the establishment
of the kingdom of the Lord; and this to Obadiah (*v.* 21)
as to all the O.T. prophets was ' the one Divine Event
to which the whole creation moves ' and for which
their hearts yearned with the intensest longing.

Further, when the prophet recognized that the unity
of the tribes was intended by God as an outward
witness to the essential inward unity of mankind ' made
in God's image' he delighted to think of a united
Israel (*v.* 20) once more bearing its clear witness, un-
dimmed by divisions which in former days had rendered it ineffectual. And it is also probable that the
prophet realized how the age-long hostility between

Israel and Edom had been obscuring that for which
the twin nations had been born, namely to bear witness
to the original constitution of the human race as one
family under the Divine Fatherhood of God (*v.* 16)
bound together by ties of love without one thought of
hatred or even animosity. This thought seems to be
implicit in the reference to the brotherly tie between
Israel and Edom (*v.* 10) which had been so outrage-
ously abused all through the ages. When Edom had
learnt through discipline and defeat no longer to
rely on her inaccessible strongholds, her worldly
alliances and her own shrewd wisdom (*vv.* 3, 4) and
to trust God as her All-Sovereign Ruler and Father,
then would be ushered in the period when the kingdom
shall be shewn to be the Lord's (*v.* 21).

What the prophet hoped for and saw but dimly
being enacted in the march of events on the stage of
human history has found its fulfilment in Christ
(Rev. xix. 10). Jesus, the Son of God, fulfilled it in
His Kingdom, which He revealed as extending over
all nations, tongues and languages—a kingdom which
knows no limits of time or space and recognizes no
distinction of race. This is 'the day of the Lord' to
which he (*v.* 15) with the rest of the old prophets
looked forward—a day which will find its complete
fulfilment when His earthly bride, typified by Mount
Zion (*vv.* 17, 21) and embodied in His Church, will be
received into heaven itself not having spot or wrinkle
or any such thing and 'God will be all in all.'

THE

BOOK OF OBADIAH

1–6. An early prophecy against Edom quoted.

THE vision of Obadiah.   1

Thus saith the Lord GOD concerning Edom: We

---

1. The vision of Obadiah. This is the title of the whole
prophecy. The same Hebrew word is found at the head of
the prophecies of Isaiah and Nahum. This title may be
from the pen of the original author or of one of his editors.
The word is a technical one for prophecy and implies a
communication from God received in the ecstatic state.
For instances of prophetic ecstasy see Num. xxiv. 3–24;
1 Sam. iii. 4–14, x. 5, 6, 10, 11, xix. 23, 24; 2 Sam. vii.
4–17; Is. vi.; Jer. i. 11–13; Ezek. i. 3–28; Dan. vii.–xii.;
Amos vii. 1–9, viii., ix. 1–10; Hab. i. 1, ii. 2, 3; Zech.
i. 8–21, ii., iii., iv., v., vi.; cf. 2 Cor. xii. 1–9; Gal. i. 12,
ii. 2, iii. 3; Rev. i. 10 ff. The characteristic of the prophets
was that they were *conscious* of personal intercourse with
God to a marked degree and so gained a personal knowledge of God's will (see Amos iii. 7). God left not Himself
without witness of His providential care and guardianship
of all men (see Acts xiv. 17), yet He chose certain persons
to be conscious instruments in declaring His Will (cf. Acts
x. 41). The wish of Moses as expressed in Num. xi. 29 and
the prophecy of Joel (ii. 28, 29) found fulfilment in the outpouring of the Holy Spirit on the Day of Pentecost (Acts
ii. 17–21). The privilege of this consciousness is now offered
to all men through the power and abiding presence of the
Holy Spirit, who enables men to appreciate with greater
ability God's character and will as revealed in Christ (see
John xiv. 17, 26).

the Lord God. The pre-massoretic text is 'My Lord
Yahweh,' or perhaps Adonay Yahweh, a proper name, an
expression which emphasizes Jehovah's sovereignty and is
very frequent in the prophetical writings. The thought of
God as the Supreme Ruler and King of men underlies the
whole of the O.T. It receives explicit mention in the last
verse of the prophecy. The massoretic traditional reading

H.   4

have heard tidings from the Lord, and an ambassador
is sent among the nations, *saying*, Arise ye, and let us
2 rise up against her in battle. Behold, I have made thee
small among the nations: thou art greatly despised.
3 The pride of thine heart hath deceived thee, O thou
that dwellest in the clefts of the rock, whose habitation

---

here is 'the Lord (or Jehovah) God' which is that of the
LXX also.

Edom. See Introduction, pp. 43 ff.

1–4. For the relation of these verses to Jer. xlix. 14–16,
see Introduction, pp. 37 ff.

We have heard tidings from the Lord. The 'tidings' refers
only to the 'utterance of the Lord' in *vv.* 2–4. The LXX
reads 'I' here as in Jer. xlix. 14. 'We' may refer to either
(*a*) the prophetic body or (*b*) the people, who have heard
from the prophets what will be the outcome of this alliance
against Edom.

an ambassador is sent among the nations. The LXX
translates by a word which elsewhere means 'fortification,'
which is probably the result of the misreading of the
Hebrew word. There may be a corruption in the LXX
text itself. Bewer suggests that the original Greek word
was one meaning 'one who rides around.' In the LXX
the mission is referred to the Lord God. 'An ambassador'
may be collective for ambassadors. The object of the
mission is to persuade various (unnamed) nations to form
an offensive alliance against Edom.

2. Behold, I have made thee small. These are the open-
ing words of 'The Lord's Oracle.' The statement may refer
to the past, or by a well-known Hebrew idiom, 'the prophetic perfect,' it may refer to the future. In the latter case
the meaning will be 'Behold, I will make thee small.'
Again, 'small' may refer to the extent of Edom's territory.
The next clause, however, favours the reference to Edom's
insignificance in the estimation of the nations.

3. the clefts of the rock. The expression occurs again
only in the Song of Songs (ii. 14). It denotes places of con-
cealed protection. The Hebrew word used for 'rock' is
identical with Sela the capital of Edom mentioned in
2 Kings xiv. 7; Is. xvi. 1 and possibly Judges i. 36. The
reference may be either to the capital or to the rocks of
Mount Seir. The capital of the Nabataeans who in later
days dispossessed the Edomites was called Petra which

is high; that saith in his heart, Who shall bring me
down to the ground? Though thou mount on high 4
as the eagle, and though thy nest be set among the
stars, I will bring thee down from thence, saith the
LORD. If thieves came to thee, if robbers by night, 5

---

also means 'a rock' or 'stone.' It is disputed whether the
two capitals occupied the same site.

that saith in his heart: i.e. thinketh. To the Hebrew
mind the heart is the seat of the intellect as well as of the
emotions.

Who shall bring me down to the ground? For a similar
defiant thought see Is. xiv. 13–15.

4. the eagle. The bird indicated is rather the griffon-
vulture. It has been described as 'a majestic bird, most
abundant and never out of sight whether on the mountains
or the plains of Palestine. Everywhere it is a feature in the
sky, as it circles higher and higher, till lost to all but the
keenest sight, and then rapidly swoops down again.' The
soaring habit of this bird is again noticed in Job xxxix. 27;
Prov. xxiii. 5 and Is. xl. 31.

**though thy nest be set among the stars, I will bring thee
down.** For a similar idea cf. Amos ix. 2, 3; Is. xiv. 13;
Jer. li. 53; Ps. cxxxix. 8–10; St Matt. xi. 23. 'Nest set
among the stars' is a hyperbole.

saith the Lord. Better, ('Tis) Jehovah's whisper! This
is a frequent interjection in all the prophetical books, except Habakkuk and Jonah. It is used of 'a revelation heard
quietly by the mental ear' (Driver).

Verses 5–7 are either a continuation of the earlier prophecy of *vv.* 1–4 (see Introduction, p. 37) or more probably are the later prophet's comment on the earlier prophecy as receiving fulfilment in his own day in the expulsion
of the Edomites from their territory by the Nabataeans
about the 5th century B.C. In doing so he continues to
borrow some of the terms of the earlier prophecy. It will
be observed that the corresponding passage in Jeremiah
(xlix. 9, 10) does not occur *after* (as in Obadiah) but *before*
the longer quotation (Jer. xlix. 14–16).

5. If thieves came to thee. Better, If thieves had come
to thee. The argument of *vv.* 5–7 is that the disaster
which has befallen Edom is no light one. It is not as if
neighbouring peoples had made a small foray on Edom; it
is a staggering blow; allies have acted treacherously and

(how art thou cut off!) would they not steal till they
had enough? if grapegatherers came to thee, would
6 they not leave some gleaning grapes? How are *the
things of* Esau searched out! how are his hidden
treasures sought up!

7–9. *An overthrow of Edom.*

7 All the men of thy confederacy have brought thee on
thy way, even to the border: the men that were at

---

betrayed her, in spite of her reputation for astuteness in
making defensive alliances.

how art thou cut off! is a parenthetical exclamation
expressing intense emotion.

till they had enough: i.e. just enough to supply their
wants, leaving something behind.

if grapegatherers. The figure of speech is changed from
that of a burglar to that of a gleaner after the vintage, a
very common figure in the O.T. The Deuteronomic Law
(see Deut. xxiv. 21) forbids the owner to glean his vine-
yards. The gleanings are for the stranger, the fatherless
and the widow. The same provision is found in the Law of
Holiness (Lev. xix. 10).

6. Esau. Esau was the elder son of Isaac (see Gen. xxv.)
and ancestor of the Edomites (see Gen. xxxvi. 9, 43;
1 Chr. i. 35). As in *vv.* 8, 9, 18, 19, 21 Esau stands for
Edom, just as Jacob and Joseph in *v.* 18 are synonyms
for Israel.

searched out: i.e. exposed and plundered.

hidden treasures. Job iii. 21; St Matt. xiii. 44 shew that
treasures were hidden in secret places in the ground. Diod.
Sic. XIX. 94, 95 says that places were hewn in the rocks for
the reception of treasures. Edom was on main trade routes
between Arabia and the Levant and Egypt and Syria, and
the people were doubtless very wealthy. Amos (i. 9) mentions that they were slave-traders.

7. All the men of thy confederacy. The order in the
Hebrew is different. Translate, Even to the border (or
rather, frontier) all thine allies brought thee and sent thee
off (as R.V. marg.). The allies are probably the Nabataeans.
Gen. xxxvi. 3 (cf. xxv. 13) may be understood in the sense
of an alliance between Edom and the Nabataeans.

the men that were at peace with thee. The phrase occurs
in Jer. xx. 10, xxxviii. 22; Ps. xli. 9 (cf. Ps. vii. 4) and seems

peace with thee have deceived thee, and prevailed
against thee; *they that eat* thy bread lay a snare under
thee: there is none understanding in him. Shall I not 8
in that day, saith the LORD, destroy the wise men out

---

to indicate those with whom one is on friendly terms and
exchanges the ordinary salutation 'Peace be to you.'

The resemblance between the present passage and Jer.
xxxviii. 22 is so close that perhaps both are quoting a
proverb which was in ordinary use, or it may have been a
dirge commonly used by wailing women. It is written in
the elegiac or wailing rhythm, which is called the Qinah
(or lamentation) rhythm and is prevalent in the Book of
Lamentations.

have deceived thee. LXX has 'stood against thee' which
is perhaps due to a misunderstanding of the Hebrew.

they that eat thy bread. These words are not found in
the LXX, and 'they that eat' have no equivalent in the
Hebrew. The Vulgate has 'they that eat with thee' and
the words have been supplied by our English translators
on the strength of their finding a place in the Vulgate and
other versions. If they have been correctly supplied Ps.
xli. 9 explains their meaning in the sense of 'friends.' To
take bread and salt with a person was and still is in Eastern
countries a token of the bond which exists between a guest
and his host. Byron, in *The Giaour*, alludes to the practice.
G. A. Smith thinks that the words 'thy bread' are due to a
scribal error and are not part of the original text. Bewer
suggests that what the prophet wrote was 'to discomfit
they have kept laying snares,' i.e. tripping thee up and
bringing thee to fall.

under thee. Bewer would read the Hebrew differently.
He translates it 'and thou wast dismayed.' There is no
reason for this. The Hebrew may be translated 'where
thou standest.'

The variations in the margin of the Revised Version shew
that the translators admitted the possibility of other
renderings of the verse. Nothing, however, seems to be
gained by regarding the words 'to the frontier' (border
R.V.) as the final words of *v*. 6.

Verses 8, 9. Bewer regards these verses as expressing the
prophet's belief that he saw in the overthrow of Edom (referred to in *v*. 7) a fulfilment of an old prophecy.

8. that day: i.e. the day of Edom's overthrow.

saith the Lord. See note on *v*. 4.

destroy the wise men. In Is. xxix. 14 there is a similar

of Edom, and understanding out of the mount of
9 Esau? And thy mighty men, O Teman, shall be dismayed, to the end that every one may be cut off from
the mount of Esau by slaughter.

10–11. *Reasons for the overthrow.*

10 For the violence done to thy brother Jacob shame
shall cover thee, and thou shalt be cut off for ever.
11 In the day that thou stoodest on the other side, in the

---

forecast with reference to Israel of the destruction of the
prudence and understanding of their wise men.

mount of Esau. See note on *v*. 6.

9. Teman. Teman was probably a northern or western
district of Edom and is used in the prophets often as a
poetical equivalent of Edom (cf. Amos i. 12; Ezek. xxv. 13;
Hab. iii. 3). In Gen. xxxvi. 11 it is the name of an Edomite
chief (cf. 1 Chr. i. 45). Eliphaz, one of Job's friends, was a
Temanite (Job ii. 11). Eusebius says that in his day Teman
was a town 15 Roman miles from Petra and a Roman post
(see his Onomasticon).

to the end that. This is an archaic expression. The
modern equivalent is 'in order that.' The LXX and Vulgate
place these words at the beginning of *v*. 10, 'On account
of the slaughter.'

10. thy brother Jacob. Jacob was the son of Isaac the
father of the tribes of Israel and the brother of Esau (Gen.
xxv. 26). As in Micah iii. 1 it is here used as a synonym for
the people of Judah (see Joel iii. 19). It is also used as a
synonym for the Israelites, e.g. in Amos vii. 2 and elsewhere. The violence done by Edom to his brother is
alluded to by Joel also (iii. 19) and his unfriendliness is
mentioned in Num. xx. 20, 21. For the long-standing and
bitter hostility between the two nations see Introduction,
pp. 45 f. Ezekiel (xxxv. 9) also foretold the perpetual desolation of Edom.

11. In the day. LXX reads 'From the day when,' and
Symmachus, 'On account of the day when.' Ps. cxxxvii. 7
—a psalm which undoubtedly refers to the period of the
Babylonian exile (see *v*. 1)—confirms the view that the
reference here is to Edom's unbrotherly conduct at the
capture of Jerusalem by Nebuchadrezzar in 586 B.C. (cf.
Jer. xii. 14).

on the other side. Or as in margin 'aloof' (cf. 2 Sam.
xviii. 13). The text, however, is the better translation.

day that strangers carried away his substance, and
foreigners entered into his gates, and cast lots upon
Jerusalem, even thou wast as one of them.

12–14. *Edom's unnatural conduct.*

But look not thou on the day of thy brother in the 12
day of his disaster, and rejoice not over the children of
Judah in the day of their destruction; neither speak
proudly in the day of distress. Enter not into the gate 13
of my people in the day of their calamity; yea, look
not thou on their affliction in the day of their calamity,
neither lay ye *hands* on their substance in the day of
their calamity. And stand thou not in the crossway, 14

---

strangers carried away his substance. In 2 Kings xxv.
10–20 there is an account of the destruction of Jerusalem
by Nebuzaradan, Nebuchadrezzar's officer, and the de-
portation of many of the inhabitants and the Temple
utensils to Babylon. This and *v.* 13 support the rendering
of the text against the margin which is also a possible translation. Bewer unnecessarily emends the text and translates 'When strangers broke down his bar' (cf. Amos i. 5).

and cast lots upon Jerusalem. See note on Joel iii. 3.
The religious aspect of the employment of lots is stated in
Prov. xvi. 33.

12. look not. Better, 'Gloat not' (as G. A. Smith translates) upon the day of his disaster. Job xxxi. 3 confirms this
translation. The translation of the margin is also possible.
G. A. Smith compares the use of 'alienus' in the sense of
'adverse.' LXX translates 'in a day of strangers.'

rejoice not. Cf. Ezek. xxxv. 15; Micah vii. 8; Baruch
iv. 12. Speak proudly, lit. 'make thy mouth large,' cf.
Is. lvii. 4; Ps. xxxv. 21. G. A. Smith understands the
expression in the sense of 'make thy mouth large with
laughter,' cf. Ezek. xxxv. 13.

13. The light in which mockery and exultation over
another's disaster is regarded is stated in Prov. xvii. 5 (cf.
xxiv. 17; St Matt. xxiv. 40, 45).

their affliction. LXX strangely renders 'their assembly.'

14. the crossway. LXX and Vulg. interpret by 'the
passes' (between mountains) or perhaps 'breaches' (in the
wall). The Hebrew word occurs only here. G. A. Smith

to cut off those of his that escape; and deliver not up
those of his that remain in the day of distress.

15–21. *The day of the Lord.*

15 For the day of the LORD is near upon all the nations:
as thou hast done, it shall be done unto thee; thy

---

translates 'the parting (of the ways?)' for which, however,
an entirely different Hebrew phrase is used in Ezek. xxi. 21.

15. the day of the Lord. See note on Joel i. 15.

as thou hast done, it shall be done unto thee. For the
same teaching see Jer. l. 29; Ezek. xvii. 19, xxxv. 15; Hab.
ii. 8; Joel iii. 4, 7; Ps. vii. 16, xciv. 23; Lam. iii. 64; Job
xxxi. 3; Prov. v. 22, xvii. 13. Historical instances of similar
requital are those of Abimelech (Judges ix. 56), of the
men of Shechem (Judges ix. 20, 24, 57), of the evil-doing
of Nabal (1 Sam. xxv. 39), of Joab's wanton bloodshed
(1 Kings ii. 32), of Shimei (1 Kings ii. 44), the extirpation
of Jehu's house (2 Kings x. 11; Hosea i. 4; Amos vii. 9;
2 Kings xv. 8–12), the overthrow of the Assyrian (Is. x. 7,
xiv. 24, 25), the desolation of Babylon (Is. xlvii. 5–8), and
the punishment of Haman (Esther ix. 25). This principle
of requital—or *lex talionis* as it is called—runs throughout
the whole of the O.T. and is acknowledged in the N.T. in
St Matt. xxiii. 35, 36. The law of retaliation is set forth in
Ex. xxi. 23–25; Lev. xxiv. 19, 20; Deut. xix. 21; and was
intended to be a check on the passion of revenge which is
explicitly forbidden in Lev. xix. 18; Prov. xx. 22, xxiv. 29;
and deprecated in later Jewish thought, see Ecclus. xxviii.
1–7. The law of revenge is found in the Code of Hammurabi,
and the principle was admitted in all ancient nations;
although instances of the forgiving spirit among heathen
peoples are not unknown, e.g. in the story of Pericles (see
Plutarch's *Pericles*, 5) and Phocion. Naturally it was entirely abrogated and the spirit of revenge is forbidden by
Him 'Who, when He was reviled, reviled not again; when
He suffered, threatened not; but committed Himself to
Him ·that judgeth righteously' (1 Pet. ii. 23). He 'Who
gave Himself a ransom for all' (1 Tim. ii. 6) disannulled
the principle of Lamech 'the ante-diluvian Anti-Christ'
(Gen. iv. 24) in the words of the Sermon on the Mount
(St Matt. v. 38–42), and His teaching is constantly re-
echoed by His disciples, see e.g. Rom. xii. 19; 1 Thess. v.
15; 1 Pet. iii. 9.

thy dealing. Better, thy recompence (as margin), or, thy
deeds.

dealing shall return upon thine own head. For as ye 16
have drunk upon my holy mountain, so shall all the
nations drink continually, yea, they shall drink, and

---

16. From this verse to the end the prophet addresses
his own countrymen the Jews. He addresses them as the
deputed spokesman of the Lord (Jehovah) to the end of
v. 18, and in his own person in the following verses. The
LXX does not recognize this change of address and still
refers these verses to Edom.

ye have drunk upon my holy mountain. This is a symbolical figure of speech to express the experiencing of God's
terrible punishment. The figure is found also in Jer. xiii.
12–14, xxv. 15–28, xlix. 12, li. 7; Job xxi. 20; Ps. xi. 6,
lx. 3, lxxv. 8; Is. li. 17, 22; Ezek. xxiii. 31; Hab. ii. 15;
Lam. iv. 21; Rev. xiv. 8, 10, xvi. 19, xvii. 4, xviii. 3 (cf.
St Matt. xx. 22, 23, xxvi. 39; St John xviii. 11). As the
cup produces the helplessness of intoxication so God's
wrathful visitations for correction produce bewildering
helplessness. 'The white heat of God's anger is an anthropomorphic image, but one which covers a terrible reality'
(Swete). Instead of the cup of God's fury there is now
offered to mankind the cup of suffering with Christ
(St Matt. xx. 23) and in the Eucharist 'the cup of blessing'
(1 Cor. x. 16).

my holy mountain: i.e. either Zion, cf. Joel iii. 17; Ps.
ii. 6, or Jerusalem, cf. Is. lxvi. 20. Zion, which was the
stronghold of the Jebusites, was captured by David who
made it the site of his residence. It was distinct from the
site of the Temple and lay on the south part of the eastern
hill of Jerusalem. It is often used in the prophets and
psalmists, in some passages as a synonym for Jerusalem,
in others as indicating the Temple Hill. Christians of the
4th century incorrectly used the name 'Zion' of the S.W.
Hill of Jerusalem. The usage of the O.T. and Apocrypha
and also archaeological evidence are against this identification. (See G. A. Smith, *Jerusalem*, I. pp. 134 ff.) .

so shall all the nations drink continually. LXX B omits
these words.

Instead of 'continually' some Hebrew MSS. read 'all the
surrounding nations' and some MSS. of the LXX read 'shall
drink wine.' On the strength of these various readings some
critics believe that the original text was 'so shall all the
nations drink wine.' The text as it stands, however, yields
a satisfactory meaning, if 'continually' is understood in the
sense of 'repeatedly' and not 'unendingly.' The word used

swallow down, and shall be as though they had not
17 been. But in mount Zion there shall be those that
escape, and it shall be holy; and the house of Jacob
18 shall possess their possessions. And the house of Jacob

here for 'continually' is the same as that used in the later
literature of the O.T. and in the Mishna for the 'daily burnt
offering' *repeated* from day to day morning and evening
(cf. Dan. viii. 11, etc.). There is no need to adopt Bewer's
ingenious emendation 'All the nations shall drink the cup
at my hand.' Judah's experience will be shared by all
nations (including Edom) if their conduct is such as to draw
God's wrath upon themselves. Judah is but an example of
God's method of dealing with all nations.

and swallow down. LXX renders 'and descend.' The
marg. represents the translation of a Hebrew verb exactly
similar to (if not identical with) the word in the text, meaning 'to talk wildly or rashly.' It occurs here, Job vi. 3 and
Prov. xx. 25 only. The usual Hebrew word for 'to swallow'
is somewhat similar to the word in the text, but as the word
in the text is known in Aramaic there is no reason to resort
to such explanations as a scribal error or defect of transmission, nor to emend the word to one for 'to reel or
stagger' (as a drunken man).

shall be as though they had not been. For the same
thought cf. Wisdom ii. 2; Ecclus. xlix. 9 which agree
closely with the LXX here (cf. LXX of Amos v. 5;
Ecclus. xxxviii. 11).

17. mount Zion. See note on *v.* 16.

there shall be those that escape. See note on Joel ii. 32.
The idea of a faithful 'remnant' is implied in Amos ix. 8.
The doctrine was one of the most characteristic elements
of Isaiah's teaching (cf. Is. i. 26–28, iv. 3, 4, vi. 13, etc.).

it shall be holy: i.e. Mount Zion shall be unprofaned, in-
violate. 'There shall no strangers (foreigners) pass through
her any more.' Joel iii. 17 explains the sense in which
Zion shall be 'holy' (cf. Is. xxxv. 8, lii. 1; Ezek. xliv. 9;
Nah. i. 15; Zech. ix. 8, xiv. 21; Rev. xxi. 27).

the house of Jacob. See note on *v.* 6.

shall possess their possessions: i.e. shall occupy their
former territory. The idea is expanded in *vv.* 19, 20. The
LXX, Vulg. and Targ., however, read 'shall dispossess those
who dispossessed them,' i.e. the Jews shall reoccupy their
own territory from which they were expelled by the
Edomites (cf. Amos ix. 12; Ezek. xxxv. 10). The Hebrew

shall be a fire, and the house of Joseph a flame, and the
house of Esau for stubble, and they shall burn among
them, and devour them: and there shall not be any
remaining to the house of Esau; for the LORD hath
spoken it. And they of the South shall possess the 19

---

text will bear this interpretation, which is probably the
true one.

18. the house of Jacob...the house of Joseph. See note
on *v.* 6. The thought is that of the unity of the nation in
the future under its Divine King, as in *v.* 21. The figure
of the final exaltation of truth and goodness, etc., as a fire
consuming adversaries is frequent in the prophets, cf. Is.
v. 24, x. 17, xlvii. 14; Nah. i. 10; Zech. xii. 6; Jer. v. 14;
Mal. iv. 1. The idea was perhaps derived from forest fires.
The symbol of the 'burning lake' in Rev. xix., xx., xxi. is
perhaps borrowed from this prophetic figure of speech in
conjunction with the vivid representations set forth in
Gen. xix. of the destruction of Sodom and Gomorrah. The
figure is also used of the destructive power of wickedness,
see Is. ix. 18; Ps. lxxxiii. 14; St James iii. 5, 6.

there shall not be any remaining to the house of Esau.
LXX B renders πυροφόρος, LXX A πυρφόρος. In the Lacedae-
monian army the priest, who kept the sacrificial fire alight,
which was never allowed to go out, was called ὁ πυρφόρος
(see Xen. *Lac.* 13. 2), lit. 'the fire-bearer.' Bewer suggests
the allusion here is to this custom. If the fire went out,
this was a sign of defeat, cf. the proverbial expression ἔδει
δὲ μηδὲ πυρφόρον περιγενέσθαι, 'But it was right that not
even the firebearer should escape' (Herod. viii. 6). 'There
shall not be a πυρφόρος in the house of Esau' means 'Edom
shall suffer total defeat.'

for the Lord hath spoken it. This is not the same expression as occurs in *vv.* 4, 8, and there seems no reason to
suspect that the verses immediately preceding are from an
earlier prophecy. See note on *v.* 16.

19. the South. The Hebrew word is Negeb, which is
used as the name of a district, The Negeb. LXX correctly
reads οἱ ἐν Νάγεβ and in *v.* 20 τὰς πόλεις τοῦ Νάγεβ. The
word means 'the parched or dry,' and it was so called on
account of its geological formation. Ps. cxxvi. 4 speaks of
'streams in the Negeb,' so it evidently was not waterless.
The region was south of Judah and extended from the hills
south of Hebron as far as Kadesh and from the Arabah in
the east to the coast of the Mediterranean in the west (see

mount of Esau; and they of the lowland the Philistines: and they shall possess the field of Ephraim, and
the field of Samaria: and Benjamin *shall possess*

G. A. Smith, *Historical Geography of the Holy Land*, pp. 278
–286).

the mount of Esau. See note on *v*. 6.

the lowland. Again the Hebrew word is the name of a
district, 'the Shephelah.' LXX correctly reads οἱ ἐν τῇ
Σεφηλά. 'The lowland' is specifically used of the strip of
lowland west of the Judaean hills and bounded by 'the
plain' on the west. On the north it was bounded by the
vale of Ajalon, and Wady esh Sheria near Beer-sheba is its
southern boundary (see G. A. Smith, *Historical Geography*,
pp. 201–244). In a similar fashion we make use of such
expressions as 'The Lake district,' 'The Peak district.'

**they of the South shall possess the mount of Esau; and
they of the lowland the Philistines.** After the exile of the
Jews to Babylon the Edomites took possession of the Negeb
(see Ezek. xxxv. 10, 12, xxxvi. 2), and the Philistines the
Shephelah (see 1 Macc. v. 66). A reversal of these invasions
is here foretold (cf. *v*. 17, note).

the Philistines. The LXX rendering ἀλλόφυλοι is thought
to imply that the Philistines were immigrants, which is
explicitly stated in Amos ix. 7. Caphtor, which is probably
Crete, is named also in Deut. ii. 3 and Jer. xlvii. 4 as the
original home of the Philistines. R. A. Stewart Macalister,
in the Schweich Lectures of 1911, which were published
under the title, *The Philistines*, has thrown new light on
their history and civilization. He is inclined to believe that,
as the inventors of the alphabet, the Philistines 'laid the
foundation stone of civilization' and in the 'long and
stubborn fight with the Philistines for the possession of the
Promised Land'...'the Hebrews learned the lessons of
culture which they needed for their own advancement.'
He doubts whether in the light of our new knowledge the
colloquial use of Philistine for a boorish and bucolically-
minded person is justified.

the field of Ephraim. LXX translates, Mount Ephraim.
It was the northern section of the central mountain range.

the field of Samaria. Better, the territory of Samaria.
Samaria was the district surrounding Mount Ephraim. The
southern frontier was near the Vale of Ajalon, and the
northern boundary was the plain of Esdraelon from the
Sharon to the Jordan, in all about 1400 square miles, 'the
size of an average English shire' (G. A. Smith).

Gilead. And the captivity of this host of the children 20

Benjamin. Benjamin is specially mentioned in connexion with restored Israel in Jer. xvii. 26, xxxii. 44, xxxiii. 13. The territory of Benjamin lay between Judah and Ephraim. It was the tribe from which Israel's first king, Saul, was chosen. Bewer emends to 'bene-ammon,' i.e. the Ammonites, and quotes Jer. xlix. 1, 2 in support of an Ammonite occupation of the territory of Gad (i.e. Gilead).

Gilead. The name of the territory on the east of the Jordan. If the same district is referred to in Hos. vi. 8, xii. 11, that prophet seems to regard Gilead as an integral part of the kingdom of Israel. In the days of Pekah Gilead was overrun by Tiglath-pileser, King of Assyria, and its inhabitants sent into exile to Assyria (2 Kings xv. 29). The promise that 'Benjamin shall possess Gilead' may be an allusion to this disaster. In Maccabaean days (see 1 Macc. v.; Josephus, *Antiq.* XIII. 3. 1; *Wars* IV. 2) many cities in the country of Gilead were recovered by the Jews.

Bewer considers that 'the house of Jacob' (*v.* 18) is the subject of this verse. He translates 'And they (i.e. the house of Jacob) shall possess the Negeb, i.e. Mount Esau, and the Shephelah, i.e. the Philistines, and they shall possess Mount Ephraim, i.e. the fields of Samaria, and the Ammonites, i.e. Gilead.' The verse translated as in the R.V. yields the same sense without the grammatical construction being strained.

20. The meaning of this verse seems to be that, whilst the exiles of northern Israel shall again inherit their northern territory, the exiles of Jerusalem shall inherit the cities of the Negeb. Zarephath was a town on the coast south of Sidon. It is mentioned in 1 Kings xvii. 9, 10 as the place to which Elijah resorted during the three years' drought. In N.T. times it was known as Sarepta (see St Luke iv. 26) and is probably represented by the modern Surafend. Sepharad is mentioned here only in the O.T. In the Inscriptions of Darius Hystaspis a place named Sparda is mentioned in Asia Minor. In the Assyrian Inscriptions also mention is made of a place called Saparda in the S.W. of Media. The choice seems to lie between these two places. Unless this verse is part of a later appendix added after the Jews' return from Babylon the Median Saparda is probably the place intended, for Nebuchadrezzar did not conquer Asia Minor and so it is hard to believe that he transported Jews thither. The LXX renders 'Ephratha' which is the name of the place near Bethel where Rachel

of Israel, which are *among* the Canaanites, *shall possess* even unto Zarephath; and the captivity of Jerusalem, which is in Sepharad, shall possess the cities of the
21 South. And saviours shall come up on mount Zion to

---

died and was buried (Gen. xxxv. 16, 19, xlviii. 7). Bethlehem is also called Ephratha in Micah v. 1 and Ruth iv. 11. In Ps. cxxxii. 6 mention is also made of an Ephratha on the border of Judah and Benjamin, near Kirjath-jearim. In view of the fact that the other Greek versions agree with the Hebrew the LXX rendering of Sepharad puzzled Jerome, who was taught by his Jewish instructor to identify Sepharad with Bosphorus, to which place the Roman Emperor Hadrian (117–137 A.D.) removed the Jewish captives. Cyril of Alexandria in his commentary on the 12 Prophets also mentions this identification.

In the Targum of Jonathan Sepharad is identified with Spain. From this identification arose the practice of distinguishing the Spanish Jews as Sephardim, whilst the German Jews are known as Ashkenazim from Jer. li. 27 (cf. Gen. x. 3; 1 Chron. i. 6).

the captivity of this host. LXX renders 'And of the restored exiles this (shall be) the dominion. To the Children of Israel, the land of the Canaanites as far as Zarephath, and the restored exiles of Jerusalem as far as Ephratha.' This, however, is an interpretation rather than a translation of the Hebrew. Bewer emends the Hebrew word for 'host' to the name of a place, Halah, to which Shalmaneser the Assyrian deported some of the Israelites (see 2 Kings xvii. 6, xviii. 11). This seems unnecessary. If we adopt the margin 'this fortress' the reference is to Zion or Jerusalem (cf. Ps. xlviii. 13, cxxii. 7).

which are among the Canaanites. Better (as margin), 'Shall possess that which belonged to the Canaanites, even unto Zarephath.'

the South. See note on *v.* 19.

21. And saviours shall come up. Better, 'And they shall go up as saviours to Mount Zion' (so Bewer following Symmachus and the Vulgate), i.e. the exiles of northern Israel shall assist their brethren of the south in punishing Edom.

LXX reads 'And as escaped ones (cf. LXX of *v.* 14) they shall go up from Mount Zion.'

to judge: i.e. to execute judgement by punishment and so vindicate the honour of the Lord (Jehovah).

judge the mount of Esau; and the kingdom shall be
the LORD's.

---

the mount of Esau. Cf. note on *v.* 6.

the kingdom shall be the Lord's. This is the final consummation to which all the writers of the O.T. and N.T.
look. The kingdom is not to be understood only as the
establishing of an outward order sometime *in the future.*
It is the recognition of an Unseen King who *at the present
time* ruleth in the kingdom of men (see Dan. v. 21) in spite
of much opposition and wilfulness on the part of His
creatures. The time will come when that opposition will be
completely removed, and the Unseen King will be revealed
in an unprecedented way. To this glorious day—the day
of the Lord—Hebrew prophets and Christian disciples both
look forward (see 1 Cor. xv. 24; Rev. xi. 15, xix. 6; cf.
St Luke i. 33). Israel was chosen and appointed as a
witness to the unity and supremacy of God's Kingship over
men (see Is. xliii. 9–13, xliv. 6–8). So long as the kingdom
remained divided, this witness was marred. This is implied
in the prophecy (see note on *v.* 18). The Church of Christ
has succeeded to this office of witness (see Acts i. 8) and its
unity is essential for the effectiveness of its witness. For
the important bearing of the concluding words of Obadiah
on the teaching of the prophecy, see Introduction, pp. 47 f.

THE

BOOK OF JONAH

INTRODUCTION

§ 1. THE PROPHET JONAH.

According to 2 Kings xiv. 25 a prophet named
Jonah lived in—if not before—the days of Jeroboam
II. He also is called 'the son of Amittai' as in Jon.
i. 1. The 'Jonah' of 2 Kings xiv. 25 is said to be 'of
Gath-ḥepher' which, we learn from Josh. xix. 13,
was within the territory assigned to the children of
Zebulun. Gath-ḥepher is thought to be identical in
position with the modern village of El-Meshḥed about
3 miles N.E. of Nazareth, not far from Cana of Galilee
(see G. A. Smith, *Historical Geography of the Holy
Land*, plate VI). Tradition has it that Jonah was
buried here. Jonah of Gath-hepher predicted the
recovery of Israel's territory, and the writer of
2 Kings sees a fulfilment of his prediction in the
restoration effected by Jeroboam II.

There is every reason for thinking that the prophet
Jonah of 2 Kings xiv. 25 and the principal figure of
the present prophecy are identical. The prophecy
presupposes a time when the Assyrian Empire was at
the height of its power and the days of Jeroboam II
were such a time. Jonah, according to a Jewish tradition, based apparently on a subtle use of the word
'truth' in 1 Kings xvii. 24, was the son of the widow

of Zarephath whom Elijah raised to life. This supposition is fanciful and precarious. Nothing is known of Jonah's father Amittai, except that the name means 'truth.' The name Jonah means 'a dove.' Some of those who regard the prophecy as purely allegorical interpret the name ' Jonah' as symbolizing Israel. The consideration of this point is dealt with in the next section on the Character of the Book.

§ 2. THE CHARACTER OF THE BOOK.

Is the story of Jonah to be understood literally or symbolically ? It has been said that no doubt would ever have been felt about the historical character of the book, if it had not contained the extraordinary incident about the great fish. This, however, is not the only difficulty in the way of the strictly literal interpretation. There is sufficient reason for believing that the sea contains fish which can swallow a man whole, although it is not in accordance with what we know of natural processes that a human being should remain alive three days and three nights in an animal's stomach. The chief difficulty of the literal interpretation is that it affords no clear answer to the question: What is the main spiritual lesson of the book? If it is regarded as a chapter of Jonah's life, conceived as 'a drama in three acts' in which the prophet recalls an occasion upon which he shewed persistent and unrepentant recalcitrance, it is a way of presenting teaching unparalleled in the Old Testament Scriptures. Nor is there any lesson either apparent or pointed in specific words. If it is only 'by the light of the later revelation of the New Testament that we discern the meaning of this book,' then for many centuries it was a sealed book and had no meaning for the prophet's contemporaries. This is so utterly contrary to the analogy of the other prophetical books of the Old Testament as to be unthinkable. In discarding the literal interpretation, it is not necessary to deny that Jonah was a historical character or that he did actually preach in Nineveh. Rather, it is this apparently historical incident which after the manner of a Midrash[1] is made the means through which a later writer taught an important spiritual lesson.

Symbolism has been defined as 'indirect description' (Sanday); and to describe spiritual realities no other language than that of symbolism can be employed. There is, however, another meaning which is attached to the word 'symbolical.' The Hebrew was wont to describe abstract ideas by means of concrete images. To do this he used what we call symbolical language. Any existing story—historical or otherwise—he would utilize for this purpose, paying little or no regard to the actual possibility of the external embellishments he would add. His only concern was that these details should subserve his purpose. The book of Jonah is perhaps the most remarkable instance of such symbolical writing in the Old Testament Scriptures.

There are two noticeable features of the book which strongly confirm this mode of interpretation: (1) its vagueness on certain points, and (2) its stereotyped expressions.

(1) The name of the king of Nineveh is not given.

---

[1] A Midrash is an *imaginative development* of a scriptural subject in order to set forth religious teaching. This recognized mode of instruction became very common amongst later Jewish teachers; cf. 2 Chr. xiii. 22, xxiv. 27 (R.V. 'commentary'). The narratives about Elijah and Elisha in 1 K. xvii. to 2 K. viii. 15 are instances of earlier stages in the Midrashic mode of writing.

The sins of which the Ninevites were guilty are not specified. And there is no indication of the place where Jonah was cast upon the dry land, nor are particulars given of the prophet's journey to Nineveh. Further the narrative ends abruptly.

(2) Such stereotyped expressions are 'Nineveh, that great city' (i. 2, iii. 2, iv. 11), 'rose up (hasted) to flee' (i. 3, iv. 2), 'doest thou well to be angry' (iv. 4, 9). Also compare i. 6*b* with iii. 9.

§ 3. THE PURPOSE OF THE BOOK.

It is hardly doubtful, then, that the book was written for a 'didactic' purpose, i.e. to bring home to men's consciences truths insufficiently realized or to recall them from errors in belief. Whilst there are subsidiary lessons (which will be noticed in the next section), the chief aim of the book seems to be indicated in its two closing verses. The Jew always had the strong temptation to restrict God's saving grace to his own nation. He found it extremely hard to make his own the prophetical teaching that God had given Israel for 'a light of the Gentiles.' He did not welcome the truth that 'to the Gentiles also hath God granted repentance unto life.'

Accordingly, Jonah, the recalcitrant prophet, is set forth as typifying a privileged but selfish and exclusive people. His unwillingness to grasp the largeness of God's mercy reflects a national failing which involved the great refusal of fulfilling the world-wide mission with which Israel was entrusted by God.

§ 4. THE RELIGIOUS VALUE OF THE BOOK.

The chief aim of the book has been set forth in the last section. There are other lessons which must not be passed over. Amongst these may be mentioned

(a) the great lesson of the Parable of the Prodigal Son, viz. how readily God welcomes those who turn to Him in sincere repentance. This is shewn in the case of the heathen sailors (c. i. 5—16), of Jonah (c. ii.), and of the Ninevites (iii. 5—10); (b) the lesson of the wickedness and futility of attempting to evade the work which God gives every man to do; (c) repentance on man's part may avail to revoke God's sentence and to avert His judgements even after they have been pronounced.

It is almost impossible to exaggerate the importance of the teaching of this small book and the place it occupies in the development of 'particularism[1]' into 'universalism' in the best thought of Judaism. The sublime teaching that God would have *all* men everywhere to repent and come to the knowledge of the truth carries one to the very threshold of the teaching of the New Testament as revealed in Christ. God's concern for the well-being of the heathen world, His loving pity for *all* His creatures and the underlying premiss that *all* men, as made in God's image, have that within them which is waiting to be awakened and respond to their Heavenly Father's call, are truths which can never grow old and have an abiding value for all times. No book of the Old Testament enunciates them more clearly than the book of Jonah. The reluctance of the Jews to see this truth is a melancholy fact. It is also a warning against those narrownesses and pettinesses which often prove so strong temptations to religious people and communities in all ages.

[1] 'Particularism' is a name given by moderns to the thought that Jehovah was the national Deity of Israel alone. 'Universalism' is applied to the teaching that Jehovah is the God and Father of the whole world.

Our Lord's reference to Jonah in St Matthew xii. 39—41, St Luke xi. 29—30 calls for special notice. The main difficulty which has been felt is this. Our Lord seems in these passages to regard Jonah's confinement in the belly of the sea-monster as a sign or foreshadowing of His own rest in the grave. And the main point of the parallel, according to this view, is the identity of the period 'three days and three nights.' The conclusion usually drawn is this. If the resting of the Lord's Body in the grave for three days and three nights is historically and physically true, then the confinement of Jonah in the sea-monster's belly for three days and three nights must also be historically and physically true. Our Lord Himself expressly makes one event a sign of the other event, and His authority on a matter of historical fact cannot, it is thought, be doubted or questioned even when that fact is contrary to human experience.

Many have felt that the demand made upon their faith in this matter is greater than as honest thinkers they can respond to. In order to meet the difficulty it has been suggested that Our Lord used the incident in the Book of Jonah simply as an illustration, without any thought of its historical or unhistorical character, somewhat as a modern speaker uses an illustration from a romance in order to point a moral or spiritual truth. Our Lord, so it is said, did not consider it part of His work to pronounce on matters of historical or literary criticism. Even so the difficulty about the three days and the three nights still remains. As a matter of fact Our Lord's Body was not according to the Gospel narrative actually three days and three nights in the tomb. Even if St Matthew xii. 40 is a comment of the Evangelist and not the *ipsissima verba* of Our Lord, the difficulty still remains. Professor Kennett suggests that Jonah is an allegorical representation of Israel. Israel was swallowed up among the nations of the world to be disciplined by suffering and through it was preserved by God and restored to a fuller spiritual life in order to fulfil its divinely-appointed mission to the world. This law of obedience and service through the discipline of suffering is a law of human life and will be repeatedly exhibited in the Israel of God—the Church of Christ—in all ages. It will also find its fulfilment in Him Who is at once the Head of Humanity and the Head of the Church, His Body, the Son of Man. It will be seen on this interpretation that the 'three days and three nights' represents the period of disciplinary suffering. 'As Jonah has his period of disciplinary suffering (three days and three nights) in the belly of the sea-monster, so shall the Son of Man be His three days and three nights (i.e. His period of disciplinary suffering) in the heart of the earth' (i.e. amid the temptations and sufferings and struggles of our earthly life). Upon this interpretation the difficulty of a direct reference to the time that Our Lord's Body lay in the tomb and to His burial is removed. Our Lord's object is to teach men to look for signs recognizable by the *inner* spirit of man and would discourage looking for *outward* tokens which make their appeal to the eye alone.

Man is here taught to regard outward events as of little or no value to him unless he sees in them expressions of the principles of the spiritual order. To regard them otherwise is the danger of 'an evil and sense-bound (adulterous) generation.'

There seems to be a strong rebuke implied in chapter iv. of that flinty-hearted feeling, sometimes found side by side with real religious zeal, and which was so conspicuous in some forms of Judaism, a zeal which takes delight in the condemnation of all other forms of religion. It is a case of ' the corruption of the best,' and produces a strange result. By an unaccountable inversion God's sternness and justice seem in the thoughts of such men to have evaporated into a sort of good-natured tenderness to those who as yet do not believe in Him. Death itself would seem to be better than to live under such a Moral Governor of the world. The irony of this state of mind is displayed by a telling contrast between the prophet's tender (though selfish) grief at the destruction of the gourd and his ruthless anger towards Nineveh in seeking its destruction. He can greatly vex himself because of the withering of a plant, whilst he remains unmoved at the thought of imminent destruction threatening a whole city. Self-centredness has almost crushed humanity out of the man; yet a spark of goodness remains in him. He has had 'pity on the gourd.' If one spark of affection even for a gourd remains in the prophet's breast, there is something within the range of the prophet's experience to which God can appeal which will give him some idea—faint though it be—of the largeness of God's Heart for all men, the children of His own creation. Whether the prophet rose to a higher state of mind is left as undetermined as the time when God shall graft in Israel again (Rom. ii. 23). Love hopeth all things.

§ 5. THE DATE OF THE BOOK.

The Book of Jonah, unlike the prophetical books of earlier periods, contains no lengthy discourse from the prophet's lips. It is simply a narrative of an incident in Jonah's life. The book nowhere claims to

have been written by Jonah and it contains indications
that it was not written until long after his death.
(*a*) Nineveh, which fell in 606 B.C., is referred to as a
city of the past (iii. 3). (*b*) The 'king of Nineveh'
(iii. 6) is an expression which would hardly be used
while the Assyrian Empire was still in existence.
(*c*) The style of the book and its Aramaisms are
those of post-exilic writings. (*d*) It contains what
are undoubtedly quotations and reminiscences of Old
Testament passages, e.g. compare Jonah iv. 3, 8 with
I Kings xix. 4, Jonah iii. 9 with Joel ii. 14, Jonah
iv. 2 with Joel ii. 13, Jonah iii. 8 with Jer. xviii. 11,
xxvi. 3, xxxvi. 3. The whole story of the sea-monster,
which is probably borrowed from the popular mythology of the Hebrews and not from Greek sources, is
perhaps a development of Jeremiah li. 34, 44. The
Psalm of chap. ii. has the closest affinities with many
of the Psalms in the Psalter, as the reference Bibles
indicate. (*e*) The expression 'God of heaven' (i. 9)
is, with the single exception of Gen. xxiv. 3, 7,
characteristic of post-exilic literature.

Whether the book is a product of the Persian or
Greek period is uncertain. At any rate by the time
of Ben Sira (Ecclesiasticus xlix. 10) it was included
in the Canon of the Prophets which was closed about
200 B.C.

§ 6. SEMITIC MYTHOLOGY.

New light was thrown upon Semitic mythology in
general and Assyro-Babylonian in particular when the
Creation Tablets were discovered and brought to the
British Museum from the famous library of the
Assyrian King Asshurbanipal (668–626 B.C.), which
was excavated at Kouyunjik, the ancient Nineveh,
some forty to fifty years ago. These tables are inscribed

in the cuneiform (i.e. wedge-shaped) writing, and give
an Assyro-Babylonian account of the Creation. Whilst
their differences from the account in Genesis are very
marked, on the other hand the resemblances are so
close as to leave little doubt that Assyro-Babylonian
mythology has had some influence upon the Old
Testament. Dr Johns describes myths as 'primitive
attempts to put an hypothesis into words before
language has become sufficiently developed for
scientific terms to be available.' All nations have
their mythological stage, and resemblance in myths
need not imply dependence. It has been said that
'men everywhere on reaching the same stage of
civilization arrive at much the same solution of the
same problems, moral, intellectual, industrial, or
religious.' Be this as it may, the 'colouring' (so to
speak) of the Assyro-Babylonian myths bears so close
a hue to language used by O.T. writers as to suggest
intimate connexion. Babylonian mythology had its
conceptions of sea-monsters, as the figure set forth in
Jonah, and of dragons. For such a physical pheno-
menon as an eclipse recourse was had to metaphor,
and a dragon was said to devour the sun. The expression was apparently not regarded as stating a literal
fact, any more than such a statement as occurs in
Ps. xiv. 4, 'Who eat up my people as they eat bread.'

The allusions to Leviathan (Job iii. 8, xli. 1; Ps.
lxxiv. 14, civ. 26; Is. xxvii. 1), to Rahab (Job ix. 13,
xxvi. 17; Ps. lxxxix. 11, Is. li. 9), to Behemoth (Job
xl. 15), to the great dragon (Is. xxvii. 1, li. 9; Ezek.
xxix. 3, xxxii. 2) are apparently allusions to Hebrew
mythology. They need no more imply a belief in the
legends on the part of the Biblical writers than is
implied by a modern alluding to figures of Greek
mythology. The O.T. poets and prophets employed

them as supporting the element of truth which they unconsciously conveyed, e.g. that there is an incessant warfare between good and evil, represented in all ages under different figures, such as light and darkness, storm and calm. The sea seems always to have conveyed to the human mind a ready figure of the powers of evil (see Is. lvii. 20; Ps. lxxxix. 9; Jude 13). The great truth which the O.T. writers bring to light is that God is stronger than the powers of evil which are always seeking to enslave His people and is Himself their Deliverer. This truth, foreshadowed in the O.T., was shewn on the stage of the present world's activities to be a fact in the life and death of Jesus Christ, the Son of God and Son of Man, in Whom as the Sinless One the conflict reached its climax and evil was finally and triumphantly overthrown (see St Luke x. 18 R.V.).

THE

BOOK OF JONAH

i. 1–3. *Jonah flees from Joppa by ship.*

Now the word of the LORD came unto Jonah the 1
son of Amittai, saying, Arise, go to Nineveh, that 2
great city, and cry against it; for their wickedness
is come up before me.   But Jonah rose up to flee unto 3
Tarshish from the presence of the LORD; and he went
down to Joppa, and found a ship going to Tarshish:

---

i. 1.   Jonah the son of Amittai.   In 2 Kings xiv. 25 a
Jonah the son of Amittai is mentioned.   See Introduction,
p. 65.

3.   Tarshish.   The situation of Tarshish is not certainly
known.   To Biblical writers it seems to represent the
most remote quarters of the earth (see Is. xxiii. 6, 10,
lxvi. 19; Ezek. xxxviii. 13; Ps. lxxii. 10).   Hence the
expression 'ships of Tarshish' (cf. our 'East Indiaman'),
see 1 Kings x. 22; Ezek. xxvii. 25; Is. lx. 9.   The LXX
translators appear to have identified Tarshish with
Carthage (see Ezek. xxvii. 12 and Is. xxiii. LXX);
Josephus (*Ant.* 1. vi. 1) thinks it is Tarsus in Cilicia.   The
identification, most widely accepted now, is that with
Tartessus in Spain, whilst some few scholars think of the
Etruscans in Italy.   It has been recently suggested that
Tarshish was a confederacy of Mediterranean islands,
including at least Sardinia and Sicily.

Joppa.   Joppa was the only seaport town on the coast
between Egypt and Mount Carmel (see G. A. Smith,
Historical Geography, pocket map).   Its antiquity is
attested by its mention on the Karnak lists and in the
account of the travels of a *mohar* or Assyrian military
commander of the time of Rameses II. (c. 1300–1234 B.C.).
According to Josh. xix. 46 it was assigned to Dan at the
distribution of the land among the tribes of Israel.   Here
timber from Lebanon for the Temple at Jerusalem was

so he paid the fare thereof, and went down into it, to go with them unto Tarshish from the presence of the LORD.

4–6. *A mighty tempest arises; the mariners fall to prayer.*

4 But the LORD sent out a great wind into the sea, and there was a mighty tempest in the sea,
5 so that the ship was like to be broken. Then the mariners were afraid, and cried every man unto his god; and they cast forth the wares that were in the ship into the sea, to lighten it unto them. But Jonah was gone down into the innermost parts of the
6 ship; and he lay, and was fast asleep. So the shipmaster came to him, and said unto him, What meanest thou, O sleeper? arise, call upon thy God, if so be that God will think upon us, that we perish not.

7–10. *The disobedience of Jonah is made known.*

7 And they said every one to his fellow, Come, and let us cast lots, that we may know for whose cause this evil is upon us. So they cast lots, and the lot fell

---

beached (2 Chron. ii. 16; Ezra iii. 7). Its subsequent history has been full of stirring events especially in Maccabaean and Roman times, and to-day it survives as Jaffa with a mixed population of some 8000 inhabitants and is in railway communication with Jerusalem.

went down into it. Or, as we should say, 'went on board.'

5. the wares. This may mean the cargo, or the ship's tackle only.

gone down into the innermost parts of the ship. Or, as we should say, 'gone down below.'

6. shipmaster. That is, 'captain' or 'skipper.'

What meanest thou, O sleeper? Better 'What meanest thou by sleeping!' LXX 'What meanest thou snoring!'

will think upon us. Or 'will give a thought to us.'

8. for whose cause this evil is upon us. These words are omitted by the best LXX MS. They are probably an addition to the Hebrew text.

upon Jonah. Then said they unto him, Tell us, we 8
pray thee, for whose cause this evil is upon us; what
is thine occupation? and whence comest thou? what
is thy country? and of what people art thou? And 9
he said unto them, I am an Hebrew; and I fear the
LORD, the God of heaven, which hath made the sea
and the dry land. Then were the men exceedingly 10
afraid, and said unto him, What is this that thou hast
done? For the men knew that he fled from the presence of the LORD, because he had told them.

11–16. *Jonah thrown overboard.*

Then said they unto him, What shall we do unto thee, 11
that the sea may be calm unto us? for the sea grew
more and more tempestuous. And he said unto them, 12
Take me up, and cast me forth into the sea; so shall
the sea be calm unto you: for I know that for my sake
this great tempest is upon you. Nevertheless the 13
men rowed hard to get them back to the land; but
they could not: for the sea grew more and more
tempestuous against them. Wherefore they cried 14
unto the LORD, and said, We beseech thee, O LORD,
we beseech thee, let us not perish for this man's life,
and lay not upon us innocent blood: for thou, O LORD,
hast done as it pleased thee. So they took up Jonah, 15

---

what is thine occupation? Some would translate,
'What is thy business (here on this ship), i.e. for what
purpose are you making this voyage?'

9. the God of heaven. This title of Jehovah is especially
frequent in post-exilic times. It served to emphasize the
all-sovereignty of God and His transcendence.

14. for this man's life. That is to say, if we take away
this man's life by throwing him overboard as he suggests.

lay not upon us innocent blood. That is to say, Do not
hold us guilty of wantonly taking life. See Deut. xxi. 1–9.

for thou, O Lord, hast done as it pleased thee. That is to
say, For we are only carrying out Thy declared will (see
v. 12).

and cast him forth into the sea: and the sea ceased
16 from her raging. Then the men feared the LORD
exceedingly; and they offered a sacrifice unto the
LORD, and made vows.

17. *Jonah swallowed by a great fish.*

17 And the LORD prepared a great fish to swallow up
Jonah; and Jonah was in the belly of the fish three
days and three nights.

ii. 1–9. *Jonah's prayer.*

2 Then Jonah prayed unto the LORD his God out of the
2 fish's belly. And he said,
   I called by reason of mine affliction unto the LORD,
   And he answered me;
   Out of the belly of hell cried I,
   And thou heardest my voice.
3   For thou didst cast me into the depth, in the heart
        of the seas,
   And the flood was round about me;
   All thy waves and thy billows passed over me.
4   And I said, I am cast out from before thine eyes;
   Yet I will look again toward thy holy temple.

-----

17. a great fish. The kind of fish is unspecified in the
original Hebrew. The N.T. τὸ κῆτος 'whale' of St Matt. xii.
40 is only an interpretation. LXX here is κήτει μεγάλῳ.

ii. 2. the belly of hell. Rather, the underworld.
Sheôl was the term by which the Hebrew expressed the
place to which men go at death. Three different ideas
have been attached to the word on the grounds of etymology
(1) from a root meaning 'to demand.' So the place which
claims all for itself: this is improbable. (2) from a root
meaning 'to be hollow.' So the cavern: (3) from a root
with the combined meanings of 'wide gaping' and 'deep
sinking.' So the subterranean cavity.

4. Yet I will look again. Theodotion's translation

The waters compassed me about, even to the soul; 5
The deep was round about me;
The weeds were wrapped about my head.
I went down to the bottoms of the mountains;   6
The earth with her bars *closed* upon me for ever:
Yet hast thou brought up my life from the pit,
   O LORD my God.
When my soul fainted within me, I remembered 7
   the LORD:
And my prayer came in unto thee, into thine holy
   temple.
They that regard lying vanities   8
Forsake their own mercy.

'How shall I look again' seems to suit the context better.
The verse has been taken to mean: Although I am cast
out of the land of the living, yet I will offer up my prayer.
The phrase 'to look toward thy holy temple' on this
interpretation is regarded as a poetical equivalent for
praying (cf. *v.* 7 and 1 Kings viii. 35, 38).

6. The earth with her bars. The earth seems to be
pictured as a house which is shut and barred against
Jonah.

hast thou brought up. The prayer is said in *v.* 1 to be
uttered 'out of the fish's belly.' But this verse seems
to imply that Jonah has been already released from his
strange prison. The prophet is either recalling some
previous experience which assured him of deliverance from
his present plight, or his hope in God's deliverance was so
steadfast that he spoke of it as already accomplished.

the pit. The word is almost synonymous with Sheôl
(*v.* 2). Some, deriving it from a different root, would
translate 'destruction' or 'corruption' (see R.V. marg.).

7. fainted. Perhaps rather, 'grew weak.' Man's neces-
sity is God's opportunity. The past tense is to be explained
as the past tense in *v.* 6 *b*.

8. lying vanities. Although the words are used of
idols (e.g. Deut. xxxii. 21), they may be understood here
in the widest possible sense, denoting any object which
receives the worship due to God alone.

their own mercy. A beautiful synonym for God;
cf. Ps. cxliv. 2. The Hebrew word means 'love which

9   But I will sacrifice unto thee with the voice of
     thanksgiving;
     I will pay that which I have vowed.
     Salvation is of the LORD.

10. *The fish disgorges Jonah.*

10 And the LORD spake unto the fish, and it vomited out
   Jonah upon the dry land.

iii. 1–3. *Jonah sent a second time to Nineveh.*

3   And the word of the LORD came unto Jonah the
2 second time, saying, Arise, go unto Nineveh, that
   great city, and preach unto it the preaching that I
3 bid thee. So Jonah arose, and went unto Nineveh,
   according to the word of the LORD. Now Nineveh
   was an exceeding great city, of three days' journey.

4–9. *The king and people of Nineveh repent at the preaching of Jonah.*

4 And Jonah began to enter into the city a day's
  journey, and he cried, and said, Yet forty days, and
5 Nineveh shall be overthrown. And the people of
  Nineveh believed God; and they proclaimed a fast,

---

shews itself in kindness.' God's love, however, necessarily
partakes of the nature of 'mercy.'

iii. 3. an exceeding great city. The Hebrew idiom
(see R.V. marg. 'a city great unto God') is strange to
western ears; cf. Gen. x. 9, xxiii. 6; Acts vii. 20 marg.
G. A. Smith, however, translates 'a city great before God.'

of three days' journey. Herodotus v. 53 says that
'one day's journey' was estimated at 150 stadia, i.e.
about 18 English miles. It is uncertain whether the
reference is to the city's diameter or circumference.
G. A. Smith says 'to judge from the ruins which still
cover the ground, the circumference must have been about
sixty miles.' This area includes the present Kouyunjik,
Minrud, Khorsabad and Balawat.

4. forty days. The best LXX MS. has 'three days.'

and put on sackcloth, from the greatest of them even
to the least of them.   And the tidings reached the 6
king of Nineveh, and he arose from his throne, and
laid his robe from him, and covered him with sackcloth, and sat in ashes.   And he made proclamation 7
and published through Nineveh by the decree of the
king and his nobles, saying, Let neither man nor beast,
herd nor flock, taste any thing: let them not feed,
nor drink water: but let them be covered with sack- 8
cloth, both man and beast, and let them cry mightily
unto God: yea, let them turn every one from his evil
way, and from the violence that is in their hands.
Who knoweth whether God will not turn and repent, 9
and turn away from his fierce anger, that we perish
not?

10. *God's gracious acceptance of Nineveh's repentance.*

And God saw their works, that they turned from 10
their evil way; and God repented of the evil,
which he said he would do unto them; and he did
it not.

---

7. beast. The reference is to domestic animals.

7–9. The words of the decree according to the Hebrew
text occupy these three verses.   In the LXX, however, it
is restricted to *v.* 7, the remainder being narrative.

9. Who knoweth...repent. The same expression is found
verbatim in Joel ii. 14.

10. This verse is an adaptation of human language to
set forth a divine truth which lends itself to no adequate
mode of expression.   Contrast the statement in Num.
xxiii. 19, James i. 17 with that here and in Gen. vi. 6,
Ex. xxxii. 14; cf. Mal. iii. 6 and especially Jer. xviii. 7, 8.

V. 5 represents the fast etc. as beginning immediately
upon Jonah's arrival in Nineveh, whereas *vv.* 7, 8 would
seem to imply that it followed somewhat later after the
royal proclamation had been published.   The statement
in *v.* 5 may be anticipatory, unless the whole book is to be
understood as a parable, see Introduction, pp. 66 ff.

iv. 1–4. *Jonah's ill-natured displeasure.*

4 But it displeased Jonah exceedingly, and he was
2 angry. And he prayed unto the LORD, and said,
I pray thee, O LORD, was not this my saying, when
I was yet in my country? Therefore I hasted to flee
unto Tarshish: for I knew that thou art a gracious
God, and full of compassion, slow to anger, and plen-
3 teous in mercy, and repentest thee of the evil. Therefore now, O LORD, take, I beseech thee, my life from
4 me; for it is better for me to die than to live. And
the LORD said, Doest thou well to be angry?

---

iv. Different reasons have been assigned to Jonah's
anger (1) because his prophecy (iii. 4) has been falsified
(see Deut. xviii. 21, 22), or (2) because he was aware of
God's lovingkindness (iv. 2), and in a fit of ill-natured
pique even desired that God's mercy should not be
extended to the heathen. Faber has beautifully said

> 'The Love of God is broader
> Than the measures of man's mind;
> And the Heart of the Eternal
> Is most wonderfully kind':

but we make His Love too narrow by false limits of our
own. Perhaps both elements were present in his anger.
A third reason has been offered, viz. Jonah felt that if
God's threat were not carried out, the honour of the
Almighty would be lowered in men's estimation.

2. was not this my saying...country? That is to say,
Was not this exactly what I said would happen while
I was in my own country?

Therefore I hasted to flee. Rather, I anticipated things
and fled. Jonah confesses that he evaded his duty by the
ignoble means of flight.

thou art a gracious God...evil. See note on Joel ii. 13.

3. take, I beseech thee, my life. The same request
was made by Moses (Num. xi. 15) and by Elijah (1 Kings
xix. 4).

4. Doest thou well to be angry? The LXX translates
'Art thou very angry?' (see R.V. marg.), and G. A. Smith
regards it as the right translation of the Hebrew here.
A third interpretation has been offered, viz. 'Does (my)
doing good (i.e. in sparing Nineveh) make thee angry?'

5–9. *Jonah's pity on the gourd.*

Then Jonah went out of the city, and sat on the east 5
side of the city, and there made him a booth, and sat
under it in the shadow, till he might see what would
become of the city. And the Lord God prepared a 6
gourd, and made it to come up over Jonah, that it
might be a shadow over his head, to deliver him from
his evil case. So Jonah was exceeding glad because
of the gourd. But God prepared a worm when the 7
morning rose the next day, and it smote the gourd,
that it withered. And it came to pass, when the sun 8
arose, that God prepared a sultry east wind; and the

---

cf. St Matt. xx. 15. The words are then a reproof rather
than 'a soft sarcasm.'

5. a booth. Probably of interwoven boughs. Such
booths were erected at the Harvest Festival called the
Feast of Booths (or Tabernacles), see Lev. xxiii. 42;
Deut. xvi. 13, 16. Compare St Peter's suggestion on the
spurs of Hermon (St Matt. xvii. 4).

6. a gourd. The Hebrew word does not occur elsewhere in the O.T. A different one is used in 1 Kings xix. 5
and in 2 Kings iv. 39. It is generally thought that the
plant was not a gourd but a castor-oil tree (*Ricinus com-
munis*) or Palma-Christi (see R.V. marg.). Jerome bears
witness to the rapidity of its growth. Dr Post thinks that
the LXX translation is correct and that the vine was a
'bottle-gourd' (*Cucurbita lagenaria*), which would answer
the circumstances well. The Vulgate translates 'ivy.'

6. from his evil case. Or, from his distress.

7. worm. Probably, a vine weevil. The word may
be collective 'vine-weevils.'

smote. Or, injured.

8. sultry. This translation is pure conjecture. LXX
has 'scorching.' The Hebrew word occurs only here.

east wind. This is the well-known 'sirocco' (meaning
'east') wind. It brings a dry heat. See the extracts
from G. A. Smith's diary of 1891 given in his *Historical
Geography of the Holy Land*, pp. 68–9. The sirocco or
simoom and its effects on vegetation is frequently referred
to in the O.T.; see Gen. xli. 6, 23, 27; Ezek. xvii. 10,

sun beat upon the head of Jonah, that he fainted,
and requested for himself that he might die, and said,
9 It is better for me to die than to live. And God said
to Jonah, Doest thou well to be angry for the gourd?
And he said, I do well to be angry even unto death.

10—11. *Jehovah's tender compassion on Nineveh.*

10 And the LORD said, Thou hast had pity on the gourd,
for the which thou hast not laboured, neither madest
it grow; which came up in a night, and perished in
11 a night: and should not I have pity on Nineveh,
that great city; wherein are more than sixscore
thousand persons that cannot discern between their
right hand and their left hand; and also much cattle?

xix. 12, etc. Its concurrence with sunrise is noticed both
here and St James i. 11.

requested for himself that he might die. The expression
is word for word the same as that in 1 Kings xix. 4.

9. Doest thou well to be angry...? See note on *v*. 4.

unto death. Cf. Judges xvi. 16; St Matt. xxvi. 38.

**11. that cannot discern between their right hand and
their left hand.** The reference is understood to be to
children of tender years who naturally could not be
regarded as morally responsible agents. If the destruction
of a mere plant can call forth the compassion of Jonah,
how can the prophet reasonably be angry when Jehovah's
compassion is evoked by helpless and innocent persons,
not to mention unoffending animals? This is the point of
the main lesson enforced by the book probably in a wider
application. See Introduction, pp. 68 ff.

THE

BOOK OF MALACHI

INTRODUCTION

§ 1. THE PROPHET AND HIS PROPHECY.

It is uncertain if the name of the writer of the book is known. 'Malachi' is identical with a Hebrew word meaning 'my messenger' or 'my angel.' Of course it is possible that it may be a proper name. Certain things, however, make this doubtful. The LXX of i. 1 is 'The burden of the word of the Lord by the hand of *His Messenger*,' and the Targum adds 'whose name is called Ezra the scribe.' The word 'Malachi' occurs in iii. 1. It may have been borrowed from this central passage and used as an artificial name by a compiler. The fact that the expression 'the burden of the word of the Lord' occurs only twice elsewhere as the heading of two anonymous prophecies, viz. Zech. ix. 1 and xii. 1, strengthens the idea that this prophecy also is anonymous. These three prophecies are all grouped together in the Hebrew Canon.

By the 2nd century A.D. Malachi was understood as the name of a person. In the later Greek versions of Aquila, Symmachus and Theodotion it is so treated. Various suggestions have been made as to its exact meaning. It has been thought to be an abbreviated form of Malachiah (which, however, does not occur in the O.T.) meaning either 'Jehovah (or Yahweh) is angel' or 'Angel of Jehovah (or Yahweh).'

Internal evidence shews that the author of the prophecy, whatever his name may have been, was a patriot who combined the conviction of the special calling of Israel with an intense belief that the religious worship of the Gentiles is acceptable to God in so far as it is the best according to their knowledge and opportunities.

The English version follows the printed editions of the LXX, Vulgate and Peshitta in dividing the book into four chapters; the Hebrew divides it into three, uniting the third and fourth chapters in one. In respect of subject-matter the prophecy falls naturally into seven sections.

(1) i. 2—5. A proof of Jehovah's love of Israel. This is shewn by a contrast being drawn between the twin nations Israel and Edom. History shews that Israel has received all along in a marked degree special tokens of Jehovah's loving care, far beyond any received by Edom; although Edom was Israel's twin nation and similar treatment of Edom might have been expected on the ground of near relationship with Israel.

(2) i. 6—14. A reproof to the priests for profaning the name of Jehovah. Even the Gentiles in their ignorance (unless the expression is to be understood of the Jewish colonists in Egypt, see note on i. 11) offer worship more pleasing to the Lord of hosts than that so slovenly and contemptuously offered by Israel's priests.

(3) ii. 1—9. A charge to the priests to reform. Reformation is called for in two directions, viz. (i) the priests are to put away irreverence and slovenliness from their performance of sacrificial ceremonies; and (ii) as 'messengers of the Lord of hosts' they are to take care to instruct the people more carefully and

intelligently in their moral as well as their ceremonial duties.

(4) ii. 10—16. A denunciation of the abomination of divorce. The grounds of the denunciation are that divorce breaks the family relationship between Jehovah and His people, and so frustrates the Divine Purpose of Creation; it also brings by its perfidy the deepest sorrow into family life.

(5) ii. 17—iii. 6. A rebuke of the prevalent scepticism. A day is coming in which Jehovah will clearly shew that He discriminates between good and evil. His discriminating judgement will put to the test the moral and spiritual condition of both priest and people. Jehovah's character remains unchangeable, even at times when men by their sins render themselves unable to discern it.

(6) iii. 7—iv. 3. A call to repentance. The spiritual deterioration is shewn by two unmistakable signs, viz. (i) the people's neglect to support by tithes and dues spiritual ministrations; and (ii) the commercial idea of profit and loss (see iii. 14, 15) which had invaded their spiritual life, of seeking *temporal* and *earthly* recompense in return for serving God. Spiritual recovery is possible through faith in God as a loving Father who discerns between righteousness and wickedness. The day shall declare it.

(7) iv. 4—6. The Law of Moses and Prophecy. The purpose of the Law is identical with that of prophecy, viz. to restore to the community its true social relationships. God will never leave Himself without an Elijah to witness against the disintegrating forces of evil.

§ 2. THE DATE OF THE PROPHECY.

Two questions must be answered before we can arrive at a conclusion about the date of the prophecy:—(1) What period in Israel's history suits the circumstances which the prophecy discloses? (2) Was the Deuteronomic or the Priestly Code of the Law in force?

(1) The circumstances which the prophecy discloses are these.

The Temple has been rebuilt (iii. 1), and the sacrificial rites are being carried on within it (i. 7, 10, 13). The community is under the civil rule of a 'governor' (i. 8). The word used is the common one for a provincial governor appointed by the Persian monarchs. The three chief abuses, which are denounced, are the degeneracy of the priesthood, the practice of divorce in order to marry foreign women, the general remissness in paying tithes and other dues for sacred purposes.

Chapter i. 2—5 contain a reference to some desolation of Edom. Unfortunately our knowledge of the history of Edom is very meagre. We know that Nabataean Arabs had invaded Edom sometime before 312 B.C., for in that year an expedition was sent against the Nabataeans who were settled in Petra (Diod. xix. 94—100). The idea that Edom was laid desolate by the Chaldaeans about 586 B.C. rests on a very doubtful interpretation of some of the prophecies against Edom.

When we turn to the period covered by the books of Ezra and Nehemiah we find circumstances similar to these. The Temple was rebuilt about 515 B.C.; and Jerusalem throughout the two centuries of Persian rule was under governors appointed by Persian kings. The three chief abuses mentioned

in Malachi are identical with those with which
Nehemiah dealt, viz. marriages with foreign women
(Neh. xiii. 23—28; Mal. ii. 10—16; cf. Ezra ix. 10),
withholding the payment of tithes and other sacred
dues (Neh. xiii. 10—12; Mal. iii. 8—10), and the
degeneracy of the priesthood (Neh. xiii. 29; Mal. ii.
1—9). With iii. 5 compare also Neh. v. 1—13. It
should be noted that, while there is no mention of
divorce in Nehemiah, in Malachi no reference is made
to the desecration of the Sabbath (Neh. xiii. 15—22).

The argument from silence is open to abuse. Still
it has its proper place amongst evidence. The fact
that no mention is made of the Exile in the Book
of Malachi would seem to indicate that it was at the
time of writing an event of the far distant past. Also
the fact that instead of any utterance of judgement
upon the Gentiles they are rather regarded in a favourable light (Mal. i. 11) would seem to point to a period
when the Jews were under the rule of a power favour-
ably disposed towards them. Such indeed on the whole
was the Persian rule.

There are two more pieces of evidence which
should be noticed. The despondency verging on the
godless spirit which characterized the people of
Malachi's time was, it may well be supposed, the
natural development of the bitter disappointment
felt by some in the days of Haggai and Zechariah.
Again, in the books of Ezra and Nehemiah there are
certain prayers (Ezra ix. 6—15; Neh. i. 5—11, ix.
5—38). The spirit in which they are written is
that which gives expression to the ideas of God's
Fatherhood of Israel, His special regard for them,
His Righteousness in spite of all their affliction, and
the blessedness attained in obedience to the Law,
all which ideas underlie Malachi's prophecy.

The general conclusion is that Malachi prophesied some time during the last half of the 5th century B.C. when Ezra and Nehemiah were active in Jerusalem. Dr J. M. P. Smith says that 'the Book of Malachi fits the situation amid which Nehemiah worked as snugly as a bone fits its socket.' Can the date of his ministry be fixed more precisely? Did he prophesy before, during, or after the activities of Ezra and Nehemiah? And this brings us to our second preliminary question, Was the Deuteronomic or the Priestly Code of the Law in force when Malachi prophesied?

(2) Recent criticism has been busy with respect to the history of the Jews from 597 B.C. onwards. The following reconstruction is offered by Professor Kennett. The Deuteronomic Code was drawn up in Palestine during the exile and completed before the rebuilding of the Temple of Zerubbabel B.C. 520. At the same time the law was being committed to writing by Jewish priests in Babylonia which after successive recensions resulted in the Priestly Code. A return of Babylonian Jews to Palestine in the reign of Cyrus is unhistorical. The account in 1 Esdras iv. 5 is the true one, viz. that it was not until the reign of Darius (521—486 B.C.) that the first batch of Jews from Babylonia reached Jerusalem under the leadership of Zerubbabel, grandson of Jehoiachin a former king of Judah, who was appointed governor of Jerusalem. For the next seventy years or so there were continual conflicts between the community in Jerusalem and the Samaritans in the matter of the fortification of Jerusalem. During this period the Persians uniformly supported the Samaritans in their opposition to the Jews. Artaxerxes (465—425 B.C.), however, changed the policy

of opposition to the community in Jerusalem and in 445 B.C. sent Nehemiah from Babylonia as governor of Jerusalem, who completed the work of fortification in fifty-two days. In [1] the year 438 B.C. Ezra arrived in Jerusalem with a body of Babylonian Jews including some priests. His object was to unify the Church by introducing into Jerusalem picked Babylonian Jews. Within a short time Ezra returned to Babylonia and took another step towards the unification of the Church by amalgamating the Palestinian law books JE and D with the Babylonian law book P. In 433 B.C. Nehemiah made a second journey from Babylonia to Jerusalem and brought with him Ezra's amalgamated law book which was practically identical with our present Pentateuch. This was forthwith promulgated at a general assembly of the people and was accepted as the one standard law book for both the Babylonian and the Palestinian Jews.

A Palestinian Jew, such as the author of the prophecy of Malachi was, would hardly be acquainted with the Priestly Code before 433 B.C. If, therefore, Malachi shews no knowledge of P, 433 B.C. is a *terminus ad quem* for his ministry; and he prepared the way for Nehemiah's reforms.

There are certain important respects in which the Priestly Code shews divergences from the Deuteronomic Code. Amongst these may be mentioned the two following:—(a) In the Deuteronomic Code the priests are identified with the Levites; in the Priestly Code they are distinct the one from the other. (b) In the matter of tithes there is also an important divergence between the two Codes (see note on iii. 8).

Now in the case of (a) the language of the author of

---

[1] In Ezra vii. 7, 8 'seven' is thought to be a mistake for 'twenty-seven.'

Malachi seems to presuppose the Deuteronomic stand-point, whilst in the case of (b) the practice suggested in iii. 10 approaches more nearly to that of the Priestly Code (see Numb. xviii. 21—32). The deviation from the Deuteronomic Code may be due to the exigencies and altered circumstances of Malachi's day rather than to a knowledge of the Priestly Code. This is made more probable in view of the fact that Malachi uses exclusively Deuteronomic expressions, e.g. the Law of Moses (iv. 4), Moses my servant (iv. 4), Statutes and judgements (iv. 4), Horeb (iv. 4). Further, blind, lame and sick (i. 8) seems to be a reminiscence of Deut. xv. 21. The emphasis laid on a 'male' in i. 14 seems to be consonant with that of a code prior to the Priestly Code (see Lev. iii. 1, 6); iii. 5 also seems to point in a similar direction.

The evidence is not unequivocal. On the whole, however, it seems to indicate that the prophet pre-pared the way for the reforms of Ezra and Nehemiah. Otherwise it is at least strange that there is not the slightest allusion to any recent reform movement.

NOTE. Professor Kennett's reconstruction of Jewish history after 597 B.C. has not in all points gained universal assent. Many scholars continue to hold the following opinions: (1) The Deuteronomic Code dates from the time of Josiah, 7th century B.C. (2) There was a return of Babylonian Jews to Jerusalem in the reign of Cyrus, 536 B.C. (3) The date of Ezra's visit to Jerusalem is 458 B.C. not 438 B.C. These scholars date the ministry of Mal-achi, some, before 445 B.C. the date of Nehemiah's first visit to Jerusalem; others, before 458 B.C. when Ezra began his reforms; and others, in the interval between Nehemiah's two visits to Jerusalem, 445 and 433 B.C. respectively.

§ 3. CHARACTERISTIC TEACHING OF MALACHI.

The style of the prophecy is worthy of attention.
The prophet does not set forth his teaching in the
usual free rhetorical style of the earlier prophets.
He adopts the dialectic style of the teacher. First,
a statement is made; then, an objection is assumed
to be raised; and finally, the objection is answered
at some length, in the course of which some piece of
distinctive teaching is set forth. This method is
adopted in no less than six of the eight paragraphs
of the prophecy (see i. 2, 6, ii. 14, 17, iii. 7, 8, 13).
It is unique in the Old Testament Scriptures and
seems to be the first instance of the style which is
generally found in later Rabbinical literature.

The three chief features of Malachi's prophecy which
cannot fail to arrest attention are (1) His attitude
towards the Law; (2) His conception of Heathen
Worship; and (3) His idea of the Judgement to come.

(1) His attitude towards the Law. The earlier
prophets laid very great stress on the importance of
moral conduct. In doing so, they evidently felt that
ceremonial observance was wrongly regarded by many
as the best offering they could make to Jehovah.
In order to correct this false estimate, although these
prophets did not utterly condemn such ceremonies
as sacrifices and pilgrimages, at the same time they
did continually oppose and pour scorn upon the
thoughtless and fanatical manner in which these
ceremonies were performed; see 1 Sam. xv. 22; Amos
iv. 4—5, v. 21—25; Hosea vi. 6; Isaiah i. 11—17;
Micah vi. 6—8; Jer. vii. 21—23.

In Malachi's prophecy, however, there is a change
of emphasis. To the prophet's mind the neglect of
the observance of external rites indicated that the

spiritual condition of the people was unhealthy. God
was sending His judgements on the people not in
any revengeful spirit but in order that they might
learn righteousness (see iii. 3), that is to say, in order
that they might know Him better in His essential
nature. This was the explanation of their misfor-
tunes. The ceremonial enactments of the Law no
less than the moral obligations served to maintain
an ideal, and were means appointed by God through
which the right spirit in man might find expression.
To the prophet ceremonial was sacramental. It was
a legitimate expression of a spiritual attitude. Undoubtedly Malachi agreed with the earlier prophets
in regarding ceremonial, unfilled with the true spirit,
as an abuse (see iii. 18—iv. 2); but that was no
reason against its proper use. As a matter of fact
the outward bond by which God held the Jews
together through many centuries of trial, especially
in and after the days of the Maccabees, was (as it is
at the present time) a reverential observance of the
Law. In God's providence the later prophets, beginning with Ezekiel, fostered among the people this
reverence for the Law. They saw that it answered
to the change in the temper of the people and
would meet their requirements in the days to come.
Every good thing can be abused; and if even the
majority of the Jews have so far abused it, it must
not be forgotten that many, for example the apostles
and their first converts, although they felt the temptation to substitute the outward for the inward, by the
grace of God generally withstood it and overcame it.

(2) His conception of Heathen Worship. There
can be little doubt that God revealed Himself to
Israel according as they were able to bear it (Heb.
i. 1). Whatever may have been the nature of God's

primitive revelation, the conception of God set forth
in the various prophetic writings was adapted to the
experiences and needs of the people of those successive
periods. In the days of the monarchy stress was
laid on the relation of Jehovah to Israel. This gave
rise to the idea which modern writers call 'ethical
monotheism' which finds its fullest expression in the
writings of the 8th century prophets. His relation
to the other nations of the world, where it is mentioned,
is regarded only from the point of view of His relation
with Israel. The outlook is still a limited one (see
Amos iii. 2; Hos. v. 3, xiii. 5). With the exile, however, came a great change in the religious life of the
people. Along with this came also enlarged conceptions of God's relation to mankind. Not only was
He regarded as having relations with the hearts and
lives of men individually (as Jeremiah, Ezekiel and
many Psalmists testify), but He came to be regarded
as exercising an influence over the destinies of other
nations of the world (see Mal. i. 5). His care of
Israel is at last seen to be a witness to His universal
care of the nations of the earth. Natural Religion,
when it is not debased, is seen to be a witness to the
yearnings of man's heart for his Creator; and Gentile
Worship, if offered in sincerity and earnestness, is
felt to be acceptable to Jehovah. Such is the teaching of Mal. i. 11, unless 'Gentiles' in this passage
is to be understood in the limited sense of Jewish
colonists or converts to Judaism from heathenism
(see note on i. 11). Similar teaching finds expression
in Deut. iv. 19, and is the main theme of the Book
of Jonah. When the Gospel of Jesus Christ 'the Son
of Man' was proclaimed, it was soon recognized that
'in every nation he that feareth God, and worketh
righteousness, is acceptable to Him' (see Acts x. 35).

H.   7

The Great Commission (see St Matt. xxviii. 18, 19) is universal. There is now no 'distinction between Jew and Greek: for the same Lord is Lord of all, and is rich unto all that call upon Him' (Rom. x. 12). The Church of Christ is catholic.

(3) His idea of the Judgement to come. The conception of 'the Day of Jehovah' is common to nearly all the prophets. For the development of the idea in both Old and New Testaments see note on Joel i. 15. In Malachi the idea has become disconnected from historical events and has passed over into the realm of apocalypse and spiritual processes (see Malachi iii. 2, iv. 1, 5). The Day of Jehovah has now become an equivalent for the process of the refining of human character, wherein the evil is separated from the good. In this way shall evil be purged out of priest and people alike as dross is separated from gold and silver (iii. 3, 4). As the Sun shooting its newly-released rays bursts forth in new splendour across the darkened skies, so in the day of Jehovah shall those 'that fear Jehovah's name' gain fresh apprehensions of truth from Him who imparts His righteousness to them. They will by it be healed of their old diseases. In their new life they will feel the inspiriting power of the new life which is in them; they will have such strength as will enable them to overcome all evil both that which is within them and that which is without (see Mal. iv. 1—3). Every opportunity for moral and spiritual development is in a true sense a 'Day of the Lord' whether it comes to a nation in the day of battle or to an individual in the hour of temptation. But such opportunities have their focus in that unique event when the Lord in the Person of Jesus Christ came to His Temple (see Mal. iii. 1) or as

St John expresses it 'tabernacled amongst us' (see
St John i. 14, R.V. marg.). There is no reason to
think that Malachi saw in detail the method by which
the hope that was in him was to be fulfilled. He had
no vision of the historical incidents of the beginning
of the Christian era. But this is not to deny that
the Spirit, who spake through the prophet, was
aware of the Incarnation of the Son of God. (See
2 Pet. i. 19—21.) It seems to be in some such sense
as this that the appeal of N.T. writers to the fulfilment of O.T. prophecies must be understood.

Three Evangelists (St Matthew xi. 10; St Mark i. 2
and St Luke vii. 27) connected the words of Mal. iii. 1
with the mission of John the Baptist. St Matthew
and St Luke attribute the connexion to Our Lord
Himself. In Mal. ii. 7 'the messenger of the Lord
of Hosts' is identified with the priest in his minis-
terial capacity. In Haggai i. 13 the prophet in
virtue of his commission is termed 'the Lord's
messenger.' May it not well be that John the Baptist,
who in an unique way summed up the teaching of
the Old Testament Dispensation both of the Law and
the Prophets (see St Luke xvi. 16), and prepared
the way for the New Dispensation, is entitled to be
called by the name most characteristic of the work
of both prophet and priest? He, in his unique place
in the stage of God's Revelation to Man fulfils their
office and in fulfilling it closes it. This justifies the
use of the passage from Malachi in the interpretation
of the Baptist's work. Again there is no reason to
believe that Malachi was conscious that he was
announcing the ministry of any specific man. He
was announcing how God gives men opportunities
of preparing themselves for drawing nigh to Him
when He draws nigh to them.

In Mal. iv. 5 a Mission of Elijah the Prophet before the great and terrible day of the Lord is announced; and in the New Testament the coming of John the Baptist is connected with this announcement (see St Matt. xi. 14; St Mark ix. 11; St Luke i. 17). In what sense is the Baptist to be identified with Elijah? Is it to be a re-appearance in bodily form of Elijah? Or is it to be a reproduction in a signal manner of the Spirit which spake in the old prophet? The answer seems to be contained in the words of the angel to Zacharias, 'He (i.e. John the Baptist) shall go before His Face in the spirit and power of Elijah' (St Luke i. 17). The Baptist himself expressly declared that he was not the ancient prophet of Ahab's day re-appearing on earth in bodily form (see St John i. 21). Still he does not deny his spiritual affinity to Elijah in his work, which is indeed affirmed by Our Lord. The expression 'before the great and terrible day of the Lord come' in Mal. iv. 5 led some of the early Fathers to expect an appearance of Elijah as the forerunner of Christ's second advent (see Justin, *Dialogue with Trypho*, c. xlix; Augustine, *Tract.* in Joh. iv. 5, 6). The truth in this belief is contained in the thought which underlies Malachi's prophecy, namely, that the Lord's Coming, or rather, the realization of God's Presence in the World will be demonstrated not by outward exhibitions of force but by the agency of the Spirit working in men's hearts and drawing them into one family (Mal. iv. 6) under the loving care of the One Creator Father (Mal. ii. 10). In times of tranquillity, as in days of affliction, the One uniting Spirit will carry on His unceasing work. The prophet offers no proof for his belief. Faith provides the wings which lift men to the sublime heights of the prophet's spiritual lore.

THE
BOOK OF MALACHI

THE burden of the word of the LORD to Israel by 1
Malachi.

i. 2–5. *Jehovah's especial love for Israel.*

I have loved you, saith the LORD. Yet ye say, 2

---

i. 1. The burden. That is, The utterance or oracle
(see R.V. marg.). The phrase 'the utterance of the
word of the Lord' stands at the head of chapters ix. and xii.
of Zechariah. It seems probable that the words both here
and in Zech. xii. were added by an editor to correspond
with the title of Zech. ix. 1.

Israel. The choice of this name seems intended to
recall the people's thoughts to the privileged position of
those who are the descendants of him whose perseverance
secured for him and for them pre-eminence. They are
hereby bidden to remember that—like their ancestor
Israel 'the Perseverer with God' (as the writer of Genesis
probably took the name to mean)—they are sharers in
that new nature, which gained the ascendancy in that
ever-memorable struggle at Peniel (see Gen. xxxii. 22–32).
With such an unique privilege and advantage there is no
room for despondency and laxity.

Malachi. The name 'Malachi' is the same word in
Hebrew as is used for 'my messenger,' 'my angel' (cf. iii. 1).
The LXX here translates 'his messenger' (or 'his angel').
So also the Targum of Jonathan which has in addition
'whose name is called Ezra the Scribe' (see Introduction,
p. 87).

The LXX adds 'Now, I pray you, consider' which
occur also in both the Hebrew and LXX texts of Haggai
ii. 15; cf. ii. 2.

2. Yet ye say. This catechetical mode of elaborating an
argument and enforcing teaching is characteristic of this
prophecy. There are traces of it in earlier prophecies.

Wherein hast thou loved us? Was not Esau Jacob's
3 brother? saith the LORD: yet I loved Jacob; but
Esau I hated, and made his mountains a desolation,

Was not Esau Jacob's brother? Better, Is not Esau
Jacob's brother? (as R.V. marg.). 'Esau' here stands
for the nation of Edom, which was descended from Esau
(see Obadiah 8, 10); and of course Israel was descended
from Jacob. The contrast is drawn between two nations
not between two individuals.

saith the Lord. Rather ''Tis Jehovah's Oracle (or
Whisper).' The Hebrew expression is not identical with
that in the former part of this verse. See note on Joel ii. 12.

I loved Jacob; but Esau I hated. As Jacob and Esau
were twin brethren the assumption that they would receive
the equal love of Jehovah is natural. When the history
of the two nations is compared, it is plain that this is not
the case. History corroborates Gen. xxv. 23. From this
general fact of observation the prophet draws his conclusion
of the continuous love of Jehovah for Israel all through the
ages.

The moral difficulty of the ground of Jehovah's different
treatment of the two nations may be met by remembering
(in Driver's words) that 'God "chooses" both individuals
and nations,—not, we must suppose, arbitrarily, but
because, by His foreknowledge, He sees, as man cannot
see, that one has endowments, physical, mental, or
spiritual, fitting it better than another to accomplish the
work, whatever it may be, that He desires to have done
upon earth.' It is also well to remember that Jacob
(Israel) was chosen to higher privileges in this life. Nothing
is said or implied about the final destiny of either of the
two *in the life to come*. Further, the choice was entirely
independent of self-originating human merit. The principle upon which God gives men their endowments is
entirely beyond our ken. What we do know is that with
the help of God's grace *all* men are capable of inheriting
eternal life, and also that God's grace is not irresistible.

3. but Esau I hated. These words are probably nothing
more than the prophet's way of stating the condition
of Edom as it presented itself to his mind when he
reflects on that nation's career in history. They do not
necessarily imply what, to use anthropomorphic language,
might be called God's state of mind directed towards Esau
(Edom).

and made his mountains a desolation. The historical

and *gave* his heritage to the jackals of the wilderness.
Whereas Edom saith, We are beaten down, but we 4
will return and build the waste places; thus saith
the LORD of hosts, They shall build, but I will throw
down: and men shall call them The border of wickedness, and The people against whom the LORD hath
indignation for ever.   And your eyes shall see, and 5
ye shall say, The LORD be magnified beyond the border
of Israel.

6-14. *The priests' dishonourable treatment of Jehovah.*

A son honoureth his father, and a servant his master: 6
if then I be a father, where is mine honour? and if
I be a master, where is my fear? saith the LORD of
hosts unto you, O priests, that despise my name.
And ye say, Wherein have we despised thy name?
Ye offer polluted bread upon mine altar.   And ye say, 7
Wherein have we polluted thee?   In that ye say,

---

occasion is not specified. It is generally thought to be
the invasion of Edom by the Nabataeans rather than an
unrecorded desolation of Edom by the Chaldaeans in the
sixth century B.C. Diodorus shews that the Nabataeans
were in possession of the district of Petra—the old home
of the Edomites—before 312 B.C. For the bearing of this
upon the date of the prophecy see Introduction, p. 90.

jackals of the wilderness. The prophets often mention
jackals in connexion with deserted sites. Instead of
'jackals' the best LXX MS. has 'dwellings.'

4. Whereas Edom saith. Better, Though Edom say
(as R.V. marg.).

5. be magnified. Better, is great (as R.V. marg.).

beyond. The Hebrew may also be translated 'above'
or 'over' (as R.V. marg.).

6. my fear. Or, reverence for Me.

7. polluted bread. The word rendered 'bread' has here
the wider meaning of 'food' as in Lev. iii. 11 (see R.V.
marg.). It includes sacrificial flesh. The pollution was
caused by the light regard they had for their office, as well
as by the offering of diseased and deformed animals (*v*. 8).

In that ye say: sc. to yourselves.

8 The table of the LORD is contemptible. And when
  ye offer the blind for sacrifice, it is no evil! and when
  ye offer the lame and sick, it is no evil! Present it
  now unto thy governor; will he be pleased with thee?
  or will he accept thy person? saith the LORD of hosts.
9 And now, I pray you, intreat the favour of God, that
  he may be gracious unto us: this hath been by your
  means: will he accept any of your persons? saith
10 the LORD of hosts. Oh that there were one among
  you that would shut the doors, that ye might not
  kindle *fire on* mine altar in vain! I have no pleasure
  in you, saith the LORD of hosts, neither will I accept
11 an offering at your hand. For from the rising of the

The table of the Lord. The expression is a synonym for
'the altar' (cf. *v.* 10), as frequently in Ezekiel's description
of the Temple.

8. the blind...the lame and sick. The offering of such
animals is forbidden in Lev. xxii. 22; Deut. xv. 21.

it is no evil. That is to say 'There's no harm in it, it
doesn't matter.'

thy governor. The word is said to be a loan-word from
the Assyrian. It is used in the O.T. most frequently of
provincial governors appointed by the Persian monarchs
(cf. Hag. i. 1, etc.). It is also applied to Solomon's
governors (1 Kings x. 15) and Benhadad the Syrian king's
captain (1 Kings xx. 24).

9. intreat the favour of God. These words have been
understood as a genuine call to repentance. Some think
they were uttered ironically.

this: i.e. this unworthy and disrespectful offering.

by your means. Better, from your hand (as R.V. marg.).

accept...your persons? i.e. be favourable to you.

10. the doors. The double doors of the Temple court
(1 Chron. xxii. 3). The altar of burnt offering stood in a
court outside the Temple building. See on Joel ii. 17.

in vain. Or, to no purpose.

an offering. The Hebrew word was primarily a general
term for a 'present.' In later use it acquired a technical
meaning and became the name of the cereal oblation, as
specified under the Priestly Code in Lev. ii. The R.V.
has substituted 'meal offering' for the misleading 'meat

sun even unto the going down of the same my name
is great among the Gentiles; and in every place
incense is offered unto my name, and a pure offering:

---

offering' of the A.V. The Revisers have sometimes
experienced a difficulty in deciding when the word is used
in its technical sense and when in its general sense. See
on Joel i. 9.

11. The connexion of this verse with the foregoing is
not obvious. (*a*) Does it point a contrast between the
reverence of heathen worship and the disrespect shewn
by Israel in its worship? Or (*b*), is it to point out that
Jehovah is not dependent (so to speak) on Israel's worship
alone? The earnest worship of the heathen—though in
ignorance—is in reality offered to and accepted by Him.
The doctrine of God's acceptance of earnest and honest
heathen worship is stated in Acts x. 35 and is probably the
thought which connects this verse with the foregoing;
cf. also Deut. iv. 19. It has been thought the reference is
not to the heathen but to Jewish colonists, such as those
in Egypt, who, we know from the Elephantine Papyri
(brought to light 1907), had erected a Temple at Elephantine on the Nile with its own altar upon which sacrifices
were offered? There is a fourth possibility, viz. that the
reference may be to converts from heathenism to Judaism,
cf. John iv. 21. These two suppositions are unlikely.

The A.V. (cf. R.V. marg.) represents the interpretation
of some older expositors who regarded it as a forecast of
the Messianic age when 'the earth shall be full of the
knowledge of the Lord, as the waters cover the sea.' There
is no verb in the Hebrew to determine whether the reference is to the present or to the future.

As early as the *Didache* (*c.* 100 A.D.) the Christian Communion is connected with these words of Malachi (see
Didache c. 14). 'It (Mal. i. 11) was accepted as a prophecy
of the Eucharist by something like a consensus of Christian
opinion in the second and third centuries' (H. B. Swete).
The absence of words denoting *animal* sacrifice has been
thought to indicate the expected cessation of such sacrifices.

my name is great. LXX has 'My name is glorified.'
The reference is to the prophet's own time, not to the
future (as A.V. marg.).

incense. The Hebrew word seems to be capable of a
two-fold interpretation (1) generally, of the exhalation of

for my name is great among the Gentiles, saith the
12 LORD of hosts.   But ye profane it, in that ye say,
The table of the LORD is polluted, and the fruit thereof,
13 even his meat, is contemptible.   Ye say also, Behold,
what a weariness is it! and ye have snuffed at it,
saith the LORD of hosts; and ye have brought that
which was taken by violence, and the lame, and the
sick; thus ye bring the offering: should I accept this
14 of your hand? saith the LORD.   But cursed be the
deceiver, which hath in his flock a male, and voweth,
and sacrificeth unto the Lord a blemished thing:

smoke, e.g. of burnt sacrifices, (2) specifically, of incense.
Some maintain that incense was not introduced into
Israel's worship before the days of Jeremiah (Jer. vi. 20).

It is uncertain whether in O.T. times it symbolized
prayer in the mind of the worshipper. Ps. cxli. 2 may
bear another interpretation. There seems to be little
room for doubt that such was the symbol in N.T. times
(see St Luke i. 10; Rev. v. 8).

12. and the fruit thereof. If this word (for it is one
word in the Hebrew) is not a defective dittograph of the
following word which is translated 'contemptible,' the
· reference seems to be to the offerings to Jehovah, which
are regarded as the fruit of His Table.

13. ye have snuffed. Better, 'ye sniff at it (sc. in con-
tempt).' The best LXX MS. has 'And I rejected them.'
There is a tradition that the original text was 'Ye sniff at
me.' These words were felt to be unworthy of a place in the
sacred writings, and so the correction as we have it was
made by the Scribes. It was a so-called Tiqqûn Sôpherîm,
i.e. a scribes' correction. Prof. W. E. Barnes thinks that
this tradition has no foundation in fact and is simply a
Midrashic fancy. There is another alleged Tiqqûn Sôpherîm
in iii. 8, 9.

that which was taken by violence. Two interpretations
have been offered of this phrase (1) that which was rescued
in a mutilated condition after seizure by a wild beast;
(2) offerings stolen by force.   The latter idea agrees better
with the Hebrew word used.

14. voweth. LXX 'and he vows it.'

for I am a great king, saith the LORD of hosts, and my name is terrible among the Gentiles.

ii. 1–9. *The glorious nature of the priesthood.*

And now, O ye priests, this commandment is for **2** you. If ye will not hear, and if ye will not lay it to 2 heart, to give glory unto my name, saith the LORD of hosts, then will I send the curse upon you, and I will curse your blessings : yea, I have cursed them already, because ye do not lay it to heart. Behold, I will 3 rebuke the seed for your sake, and will spread dung upon your faces, even the dung of your sacrifices;

---

my name is terrible. Better, My name is respected or held in reverence (cf. *v.* 11) sc. How much more is it to be held in reverence by you ; cf. Ps. xlvii. 2.

ii. 1. this commandment. Or, This charge, viz. to reform.

2. the curse. Probably the curse in Deut. xxviii. 15 is referred to.

your blessings. The Hebrew word is used of: (1) new wine as a source of blessing (Is. lxv. 8) ; (2) prosperity (Prov. xi. 11, etc.) ; (3) gifts, presents (Gen. xxxiii. 11, etc.) ; (4) blessings (Mal. iii. 10, etc.).   Deut. xxviii. 2 would seem to favour the meaning of 'prosperity' in the present passage. LXX reads the singular, and has in addition 'and I will scatter your blessing abroad, and it shall not be among you.'

3. I will rebuke the seed for your sake. The LXX reads 'I am cutting off your arm,' i.e. depriving them of their authority and power (see 1 Sam. ii. 31) ; or possibly, depriving them of that part of the sacrificial victim, the shoulder, which was the priest's due (see Deut. xviii. 3). The word 'seed' is used in O.T. both (*a*) literally, of the produce of the land, and (*b*) of a man's descendants or posterity ; either of these meanings is possible here.

the dung of your sacrifices. Or, the offal of your festival sacrifices, i.e. of the sacrificial animals. The Hebrew word translated 'sacrifices' usually means 'pilgrimage festivals' (see R.V. marg.). But here and in Exod. xxiii. 18 ; Ps. cxviii. 27 it seems to have this secondary meaning.

4 and ye shall be taken away with it. And ye shall
know that I have sent this commandment unto you,
that my covenant might be with Levi, saith the LORD
5 of hosts. My covenant was with him of life and
peace; and I gave them to him that he might fear,
6 and he feared me, and stood in awe of my name. The
law of truth was in his mouth, and unrighteousness

---

with it. Or, 'unto it' (as R.V. marg.), i.e. unto the
place where it is deposited as refuse.

4. that my covenant might be with Levi. 'Be,' i.e. be
continued or maintained. Or, Since my covenant was
with Levi. The origin of the professional priesthood in
Israel is obscure. In Judges xvii. there is a record of a
Judaean who is an 'expert' priest. He is called 'a Levite'
which apparently is an official title, totally unconnected
with the tribe of that name (cf. also Exod. iv. 14). When
Solomon had built his Temple he appointed Zadok to be
priest (1 Kings ii. 35), and apparently from that time the
priests in Jerusalem were proud of their descent from
Zadok (see 2 Chron. xxxi. 10; Ezra vii. 2; Ezekiel xl. 46,
xliii. 19, xliv. 15, xlviii. 11). The 'Levites' still continued
to officiate in the Northern Kingdom until the Deuteronomic reform, by which all the country sanctuaries were
to be suppressed and the Levitical priests to share equally
in religious rights with the priests at Jerusalem (Deut. xviii.
6–8). The Jerusalem priests however were unable—if not
unwilling—to welcome the Levites, at any rate to share in
performing sacrifices at the altar in Jerusalem in Josiah's
time (see 2 Kings xxiii. 9). Consequently the Levites
assumed the position of attendants on the Zadokite
priests. In Ezekiel's day this arrangement met with the
prophet-priest's express approval (see Ezek. xliv. 10–16).
After the return of the Babylonian exiles the term
'Zadokites' (or 'sons of Zadok') disappears and the priests
invariably traced their descent from Aaron. Later however the name Zadok re-appears in the title 'Sadducee.'

It is evident from this passage that in 'Malachi's' day
the Levite was not regarded otherwise than as a full
member of the priestly body.

5. The terms of the covenant were these: Jehovah
gave health ('life') and prosperity ('peace'), whilst Levi
rendered to Him reverence and humility.

6. The law of truth. Better, sound oral instruction,

was not found in his lips: he walked with me in peace
and uprightness, and did turn many away from
iniquity. For the priest's lips should keep knowledge, 7
and they should seek the law at his mouth: for he is
the messenger of the LORD of hosts. But ye are 8
turned aside out of the way; ye have caused many
to stumble in the law; ye have corrupted the covenant
of Levi, saith the LORD of hosts. Therefore have I 9
also made you contemptible and base before all the
people, according as ye have not kept my ways, but
have had respect of persons in the law.

10–16. *Jehovah's hatred of divorce.*

Have we not all one father? hath not one God 10
created us? why do we deal treacherously every man
against his brother, profaning the covenant of our
fathers? Judah hath dealt treacherously, and an 11
abomination is committed in Israel and in Jerusalem;
for Judah hath profaned the holiness of the LORD

---

viz. on moral and ceremonial duties; cf. Deut. xxxiii.
8–11.

7. The priestly ideal is here set forth in clear and
permanent terms.

8. in the law. Better 'by (your erroneous) direction.'

9. base. Better, humiliated, i.e. in position.

had respect of persons in the law. Better, shewn
partiality in giving direction. The priests apparently
accepted bribes as in the days of Micah (Mic. iii. 11).

10. one father. The next sentence seems to shew that
the Father referred to is God.

against his brother. Divorce is an offence against the
covenant in which the One Father claims them as His
children. The unity of the family is broken and their
witness to it impaired; the bond of love is broken: the
judgement of God incurred.

11. the holiness of the Lord. The expression is capable of many interpretations, viz. (1) Jehovah's majesty,
(2) Israel, or (3) the Sanctuary.

which he loveth, and hath married the daughter of
12 a strange god. The LORD will cut off to the man that
doeth this him that waketh and him that answereth,
out of the tents of Jacob, and him that offereth an
13 offering unto the LORD of hosts. And this again ye
do: ye cover the altar of the LORD with tears, with
weeping, and with sighing, insomuch that he regardeth
not the offering any more, neither receiveth it with
14 good will at your hand. Yet ye say, Wherefore?
Because the LORD hath been witness between thee
and the wife of thy youth, against whom thou hast
dealt treacherously, though she is thy companion,
15 and the wife of thy covenant. And did he not make

the daughter of a strange god. Probably, women of
foreign religions. 'Strange' is here used in the obsolete
sense of 'foreign, alien.'
12. The Lord will cut off. Rather, May Jehovah cut off.
to the man: i.e. from his family.
him that waketh and him that answereth. The Hebrew
expression is alliterative, and seems to be a proverbial way
of saying 'every one,' i.e. guilty of this transgression.
There are many other such alliterative proverbial expressions in the O.T. The idea which underlies it is said
to be the challenge and reply to a sentry or watchman on
his rounds. G. A. Smith translates 'witness and cham-
pion.' He thinks that the LXX has preserved a hint of
the correct word in the first of the two words. The scene
is in this case that of a court of law. 'The tents of Jacob'
seems to favour the former idea, although it is not decisive
(cf. Jer. xxx. 18; Zech. xii. 7).
13. this again ye do. LXX reads 'And these things
which I was hating ye were doing.' G. A. Smith thinks
that *vv.* 11 to 13ᵃ are an intrusion, since they disturb the
argument.
ye cover the altar of the Lord with tears. The tears are
either (*a*) those of the divorced wives who in their distress
cry unto Jehovah, or (*b*) their own tears because Jehovah
will not accept their offerings.
insomuch that. The best LXX MS. reads 'by reason of
troubles.'
15. This verse is most difficult. The following trans-
lations have been offered. (1) A.V. 'And did not he make

one, although he had the residue of the spirit? And wherefore one? He sought a godly seed. Therefore take heed to your spirit, and let none deal treacherously against the wife of his youth. For I hate 16

one? Yet had he the residue (or excellency, marg.) of the spirit. And wherefore one? That he might seek a goodly seed (or seed of God, marg.).' (2) R.V. 'And did he not make one, although he had the residue of the spirit? And wherefore one? He sought a godly seed.' (3) R.V. marg. 'And not one hath done so who had a residue of the spirit. Or what? is there one that seeketh a godly seed?' (4) LXX 'And did he not do well and (is it) a residue of his spirit? And ye say What other than a seed does God seek?' (5) Vulg. 'Did not one make, and is (it) a residue of his spirit? And what does one seek, but a seed of God?'

(1) and (2) seem to mean, God as a matter of fact at the beginning made but *one* pair (i.e. Adam and Eve), although He could have made more, for God had more spirit of life in reserve. Why did He make but one pair? In order to have a godly seed, which could only be secured in this way. Thus God's action at the beginning proves that marriage is the law of man's constitution, and divorce is an intolerable breach of the law (cf. Our Lord's teaching in St Matt. xix. 4–6). (3) suggests a different thought, namely, No one, who had the Spirit of God in him, ever faithlessly divorced his wife, or men seek to have a godly offspring, do they not? That is surely a sufficient motive to keep them from the practice of divorce.

Kirkpatrick translates 'And did not One (i.e. God) make you both....And why did the One do so? Seeking a godly seed,' and explains 'The purpose of marriage was the maintenance of the race as the people of God, and this was defeated by mixed marriages and by divorce.' The LXX suggests objectors who interpose with a question. Some scholars translate 'But what about the One?' (instead of 'and wherefore one?') and understand it to be a question of objectors meaning 'What about Abraham' who put away his wife; but this translation is questionable.

Slight emendations of the text have been suggested, yielding the translation 'Hath not the same God created and preserved to us the spirit of life? And what does He desire? A seed of God' (i.e. children, cf. Ps. cxxvii. 3). Emendations without textual support cannot carry much weight. On the whole we prefer the translation of the R.V. understood as has been explained above.

putting away, saith the LORD, the God of Israel, and him that covereth his garment with violence, saith the LORD of hosts: therefore take heed to your spirit, that ye deal not treacherously.

17–iii. 6. *Jehovah's answer to the despondent sceptics.*

17 Ye have wearied the LORD with your words. Yet ye say, Wherein have we wearied him? In that ye say, Every one that doeth evil is good in the sight of the LORD, and he delighteth in them; or where 3 is the God of judgement? Behold, I send my messenger, and he shall prepare the way before me: and the Lord, whom ye seek, shall suddenly come to his temple; and the messenger of the covenant, whom

---

16. putting away. That is, divorce.

covereth his garment with violence. His garment may mean either (*a*) himself, or (*b*) his wife. Robertson Smith says that it was an ancient custom to cast one's garment over a woman in claiming her as his wife (cf. Ruth iii. 9; Ezek. xvi. 8). This custom may account for the figure of speech used here.

17. he delighteth in them: i.e. He (Jehovah) delighteth in them (the evil-doers). The loose tone of society had evidently shaken the faith of some in God's providence. They came to think of Jehovah as One who paid no regard to the observance of moral principles.

where is the God of judgement? It is an almost scornful question, implying there can be no God of justice or else He would interpose.

iii. 1. This is the central verse and climax of the whole prophecy, as N.T. writers have recognized. The expression 'my messenger' (in Hebrew mal'akhî) may have given its name to the book (see Introduction, p. 87). If this is so, the instinct was a true one.

my messenger. See Introduction, pp. 99 f. Perhaps to be identified with 'Elijah the prophet' of iv. 5. This 'messenger' seems to be distinct from the 'messenger of the covenant' of this verse.

prepare. Prepare, i.e. by clearing obstacles out of the way; cf. Is. xl. 3, lvii. 14.

ye seek. The desire for Jehovah on the part of some may be gathered from ii. 17.

the messenger of the covenant. The identification of

ye delight in, behold, he cometh, saith the LORD of
hosts. But who may abide the day of his coming? 2
and who shall stand when he appeareth? for he is
like a refiner's fire, and like fullers' soap: and he shall 3
sit as a refiner and purifier of silver, and he shall
purify the sons of Levi, and purge them as gold and
silver; and they shall offer unto the LORD offerings
in righteousness. Then shall the offering of Judah 4
and Jerusalem be pleasant unto the LORD, as in the
days of old, and as in ancient years. And I will come 5
near to you to judgement; and I will be a swift witness against the sorcerers, and against the adulterers,

---

'The messenger (or angel) of the covenant' is uncertain.
According to the R.V. marg. ('even the messenger') he is
identical with Jehovah, but in the text a distinction is made.
The prophets often look forward to a great future which
they picture in ideal terms (cf. the figure of Servant of
Jehovah in Is. xl. ff.). 'The angel of Jehovah' is a frequent
term in the historical books. The expression is apparently
used in the earlier strata of O.T. literature when it is desired
to express the direct and temporary manifestation of Jehovah in the affairs of men. This 'theophanic' angel (as
it is termed) is not mentioned amongst Deuteronomic or
Priestly writers. The 'covenant' here may probably be the
'New Covenant' mentioned in Jer. xxxi. 31, the records
of which are contained in the collection of writings now
known as the New Testament, which should more correctly
be termed 'New Covenant.' Christians from N.T. days
have recognized the potential fulfilment of the prophets'
Ideal Future in the Incarnation of the Lord Jesus Christ
and the establishment of His Kingdom.

2. fullers' soap. LXX has 'fullers' grass.' This was
apparently a vegetable alkali. The lye of the burnt ashes
of certain plants was used for cleansing purposes (cf.
Jer. ii. 22). The main industry of modern Palestine is
soap-making.

3. they shall offer. Better, they shall be offering. The
expression is that of a continuing state.

4. the days of old. Distance lends enchantment to the
view in surveying the past (cf. ii. 5, 6).

5. It is interesting to note how all the O.T. prophets

and against false swearers; and against those that oppress the hireling in his wages, the widow, and the fatherless, and that turn aside the stranger *from his*
6 *right*, and fear not me, saith the LORD of hosts. For I the LORD change not; therefore ye, O sons of Jacob, are not consumed.

7–12. Punishment for neglecting to pay tithes and dues.

7 From the days of your fathers ye have turned aside from mine ordinances, and have not kept them. Return unto me, and I will return unto you, saith the LORD of hosts. But ye say, Wherein shall we return?
8 Will a man rob God? yet ye rob me. But ye say,

---

laid the greatest stress on ethical righteousness as an indispensable element in religious living (cf. 1 Sam. xv. 22; Is. i. 11–13, 16, 17; Jer. vii. 22, 23; Mic. vi. 6–8; Hos. vi. 6).

the stranger. That is, the resident foreigner, to whom the law conceded certain rights. Kindness is frequently enjoined to 'the stranger, fatherless and widow' especially in Deuteronomy.

fear not me. In the sense of 'reverence.'

6. I...change not. This is usually understood to refer to the unchangeable nature of Jehovah; cf. Num. xxiii. 19; Ps. cii. 27; Heb. xiii. 8. Some understand it to mean 'I have not changed (in this specific particular).'

are not consumed. LXX joining the words with *v.* 7 reads 'ye do not refrain from the iniquities of your fathers.' It has also been translated 'have not come to an end,' i.e. are still the sons of Jacob the deceiver.

7. But ye say, Wherein shall we return? This question is usually understood not to be a genuine one. May it not be that in a long-continued course of neglect 'the god of this world has blinded their eyes' and so the question is genuinely put by those who have lost all sense of the claims of religious duties?

8. According to the Deuteronomic Code (Deut. xiv. 22–29, xxvi. 12–15, xii. 6) the worshippers with their households and the Levite are to eat their vegetable tithe at the feast at the central sanctuary each of two years out of three. And once every three years (i.e. in the

Wherein have we robbed thee? In tithes and offerings. Ye are cursed with the curse; for ye rob me, 9
even this whole nation. Bring ye the whole tithe 10
into the storehouse, that there may be meat in mine
house, and prove me now herewith, saith the LORD

---

third year) the tithe is to be laid up at home for the
Levite, the stranger, the fatherless and the widow. Thus
in Deuteronomy the tithe is spent partly in poor-relief
(including the priests) and partly on sacrificial feasts.

It is to be observed that the tithe on vegetable produce
is the only tithe mentioned in Deuteronomy.

In the Priestly Code (Lev. xxvii. 30–33; Num. xviii.
12–21, 25–28) certain differences should be noted, e.g.
(1) tithe is levied on cattle as well as on vegetable produce,
(2) the whole of the tithe is paid to the Levites, and they
pay a tenth of it to the priests, (3) no layman may redeem
his tithe without adding the fifth part thereof. These
probably mark two distinct stages in the history of tithes
in Israel. In the oldest Hebrew legislation (the so-called
Book of the Covenant, Exod. xxi.–xxiii.) tithes are not
mentioned (only the payment of first-fruits, xxii. 29, 30),
but Amos iv. 4 shews that it was a custom—probably of
long standing—to pay tithes at Bethel (perhaps ascribed
to the traditional promise of Jacob in Gen. xxviii. 22).
The abuse referred to here seems to presuppose the
legislation of the Priestly Code. A similar abuse is referred
to in Neh. xiii. 10–12, cf. x. 38–39.

ye rob. These words in this and the following verses
are another instance of the so-called Tiqqûne Sôpherîm
(i.e. scribes' corrections; cf. i. 13 and note there). LXX
reads 'ye attack in the rear,' 'ye trip up,' or 'circumvent.'
The original word in the Hebrew is of doubtful meaning;
cf. Prov. xxii. 23.

offerings. The Hebrew word used here is a technical
one. It means that which is 'lifted away' or 'separated'
from something else. So it is used of a contribution or
share, e.g. (a) of products of the soil such as tithes, first-
fruits, etc., (b) of land, (c) money, booty, (d) sacrificed
animal's thigh. The R.V. marg. has 'heave offerings.'
This expression suggests a rite of ceremonial elevation.
This practice, however, is very doubtful.

9. the curse. The curse is specified in Deut. xxviii. 20 ff.

10. meat. Rather, 'food,' 'provision'; cf. Neh. x.
37–39.

of hosts, if I will not open you the windows of heaven,
and pour you out a blessing, that there shall not be
11 room enough *to receive it*. And I will rebuke the
devourer for your sakes, and he shall not destroy
the fruits of your ground; neither shall your vine
cast her fruit before the time in the field, saith the
12 LORD of hosts. And all nations shall call you happy:
for ye shall be a delightsome land, saith the LORD of
hosts.

13–iv. 3. *The approach of the Day which will vindicate Jehovah's righteousness.*

13 Your words have been stout against me, saith the
LORD. Yet ye say, Wherein have we spoken against
14 thee? Ye have said, It is vain to serve God: and
what profit is it that we have kept his charge, and
that we have walked mournfully before the LORD of

---

open you the windows of heaven. That is, 'cause it to
rain' (cf. Gen. vii. 11, viii. 2; 2 Kings vii. 19; Is. xxiv. 18).
 a blessing. See on ii. 2.

 room enough to receive it. Literally, until there is not
sufficiency, i.e. it will be inexhaustible; cf. Ps. lxxii. 7.

 11. the devourer. Probably 'the locust.' The Hebrew
word means simply, 'the eater.'

 12. a delightsome land: cf. Is. lxii. 4 with R.V. marg.
The Hebrew word is the same in both passages.

 13. stout against me. The same word is used with
reference to Pharaoh's obstinate heart in Exod. vii. 13, 22,
viii. 15, ix. 35. The idea here is that of distrust and doubt
which is the forerunner of a peevish and complaining
spirit.

 have we spoken. Rather, 'talked together.' *vv.* 14–15
contain the gist of the conversation.

 14. It is vain to serve God. Or, serving God brings no
return. J. M. P. Smith aptly calls this 'a commercial
type of piety.'

 charge. Or, injunctions, commands.

 mournfully. Or, as R.V. marg. 'with outward tokens of
humiliation'; cf. Ps. lxix. 10, 11. It is the disappointment

hosts? And now we call the proud happy; yea, 15
they that work wickedness are built up; yea, they
tempt God, and are delivered. Then they that feared 16
the LORD spake one with another: and the LORD
hearkened, and heard, and a book of remembrance
was written before him, for them that feared the LORD,
and that thought upon his name. And they shall 17
be mine, saith the LORD of hosts, in the day that I
do make, *even* a peculiar treasure; and I will spare
them, as a man spareth his own son that serveth him.
Then shall ye return and discern between the righteous 18
and the wicked, between him that serveth God and

---

of those who have tried to serve God with apparently no
advantage to themselves.

15. And now we call the proud happy. G. A. Smith
translates 'Even now we have got to congratulate the
arrogant.' The word is almost a technical term for the
godless, those who practise no religion. The problem of
the relative advantage of the godly and godless was felt
by the authors of Pss. xxxvii., xlix. and lxxiii. It also
forced itself on St Peter's mind, see St Matt. xix. 27–30.

16. Then. LXX reads, These things.

a book of remembrance. The idea of a Divine register
of men is first found in Exod. xxxii. 32. It is of frequent
occurrence in both O.T. and N.T., see Ps. lvi. 8, lxix. 28,
cxxxix. 16; Is. iv. 3; Dan. xii. 1; St Luke x. 20; Phil.
iv. 3; Heb. xii. 23; Rev. iii. 5, xiii. 8, xvii. 12, xx. 12.
The prophets Jeremiah and Ezekiel refer to registers of
citizens (Jer. xxii. 30; Ezek. xiii. 9; cf. Esther vi. 1).

17. in the day that I do make, even a peculiar treasure.
Or, In the day on which I act; cf. iv. 3. G. A. Smith
translates, 'And they shall be mine own property, saith
Jehovah of Hosts, in the day when I rise to action.'

The word translated 'a peculiar treasure' is first applied
to Israel in Exod. xix. 5. 'Peculiar' is to be understood
in its strict etymological sense of 'one's own special
possession.' 'Erunt in die judicii in peculium et parcet
eis' (Jerome *in loco*). The term has been taken over
by N.T. writers and applied to the 'Israel of God'—the
Christian Church—in Eph i. 14; Tit. ii. 14; 1 Pet. ii. 9.

4 him that serveth him not. For, behold, the day
cometh, it burneth as a furnace; and all the proud,
and all that work wickedness, shall be stubble: and
the day that cometh shall burn them up, saith the
LORD of hosts, that it shall leave them neither root
2 nor branch. But unto you that fear my name shall
the sun of righteousness arise with healing in his wings;
and ye shall go forth, and gambol as calves of the stall.
3 And ye shall tread down the wicked; for they shall
be ashes under the soles of your feet in the day that
I do make, saith the LORD of hosts.

---

iv. 1. the day. See note on Joel i. 15.

a furnace. The article indicated here was a large earthen
portable stove, such as is still in use in Syria. The representation seems to be a two-fold one (1) of Jehovah's
presence, and (2) of His judgement (cf. Exod. iii. 2; 2 Thess.
i. 7, 8).

all the proud, and all that work wickedness. The words
obviously refer back to iii. 15. The judgement of the
faithless will be found to be unwarranted.

2. the sun of righteousness. The righteousness of the
true worshippers of Jehovah which will be vindicated in
'the day of the Lord' is here compared with the sun.
Cf. for the idea Ps. xxxvii. 6; Prov. iv. 18; Dan. xii. 3;
Is. lxii. 1 and especially St Matt. xiii. 43.

Their influence, like the sun's rays, will bring new
vitality and joy to the righteous sufferers.

Some have seen in the mention of 'wings' an allusion
to representations of solar disks with wings issuing from
the sides.

The verse may be interpreted in a Messianic sense, and
indeed was so understood by many of the Christian Fathers;
cf. for a similar idea St Luke i. 78; St John i. 4, viii. 12,
ix. 5, xii. 46; Is. liii. 5.

his wings: i.e. its wings. With the exception of Lev.
xxv. 5 the word 'its' does not occur in the A.V. of 1611.
It is never found in Spenser, and rarely in the writings of
Shakespeare, Bacon or Milton.

calves of the stall. It is a simile of happy prosperity
and vitality.

3. in the day that I do make. Or, in the day on which
I act; cf. iii. 17.

4–6. *The coming of Elijah the prophet.*

Remember ye the law of Moses my servant, which 4
I commanded unto him in Horeb for all Israel, even
statutes and judgements.　Behold, I will send you 5
Elijah the prophet before the great and terrible day
of the LORD come.　And he shall turn the heart of the 6
fathers to the children, and the heart of the children

4.　Horeb.　This is the name which is characteristic
of the Elohistic narrative and of Deuteronomy.　The
Jehovistic and the Priestly narratives prefer ' Sinai.'　The
identification of Horeb with Sinai is uncertain; equally
uncertain are their respective sites.

statutes and judgements.　This is a favourite Deuteronomic phrase.　In the best LXX MS. *v.* 4 is omitted here
and stands after *v.* 6.　This may indicate that it was
added later.

5.　Elijah the prophet.　Elijah was the great prophet
in Israel in the days of Ahab (see 1 Kings xvii.–2 Kings ii.).
According to the narrative in Kings he was carried up by
a whirlwind into heaven.　It is this presumably which
associated the restoration of prophecy with his name.
The belief of the return of Elijah is one which took
strong hold on Jewish thought.　It is found in Ecclesiasticus xlviii. 10, 11, and frequently alluded to in the N.T.
(St Matt. xi. 14, xvi. 14, xvii. 10; St Mark vi. 5, viii. 28,
ix. 11; St Luke ix. 8, 19; St John i. 21).

The belief is also found in the Mishna and is cherished
in Jewish thought to the present time.　At every Passover
a vacant seat is kept for Elijah as an expected guest.
Greeks and Mohammedans alike also do honour to his
name, and both the Greek and the Latin Church observe
a day in his memory.

For the bearing of this passage on the mission of the
Baptist, see Introduction, p. 100.

before the great and terrible day of the Lord come.
These words occur verbatim in Joel ii. 31.

6.　he shall turn the heart, etc.　It is apparent that
dissensions were rife which threatened the social. order,
and probably the existence of the community.　It may
possibly indicate a great upheaval of thought and customs,
such as was caused by contact with Greek life and thought.

to their fathers; lest I come and smite the earth with
a curse.

---

the earth. The reference seems to be restricted to the
land of Israel (cf. R.V. marg.).

curse. That is to say, utterly destroy it. The word
used here (ḥêrem) is the technical word for the war custom
of 'devoting' a conquered city to the deity. The whole
city was given over to the god as an act of gratitude. All
human beings were destroyed. This 'ban' was known in
Moab and probably in Assyria (cf. 2 Kings ix. 11) as well
as in Israel. It is mentioned on Mesha's Inscription or
the Moabite Stone. The chief O.T. instances of the 'ban'
are those recorded in Numb. xxi. 2, 3; Deut. ii. 34, iii. 6,
vii. 2, xx. 7; Jos. ii. 10, vi. 17–19, viii. 2, x. 11; 1 Sam. xv.

In later days the awful ban gave place to excommunica-
tion, and Ezra x. 8 is commonly regarded as marking the
transition.

INDEX